THE
EVERYTHING
GLUTEN-FREE COLLEGE
COOKBOOK

Dear Reader,

Congrats! If you are buying this book it probably means you, your child, or a good friend is headed to college. College can be a wonderful opportunity to enjoy independence, spend late nights studying, and discover your favorite hobbies and skills, as well as where you want to go in life.

As a college graduate and a gluten-free employee who works full time on a college campus, I know the tremendous challenges first-time students face. For students with celiac disease, gluten sensitivity, and/or food allergies, the challenge can be even more daunting. All of a sudden you'll have to be in charge of every meal and snack you eat. You'll have to know what's safe and what isn't. Mom and Dad won't be there to cook meals, go grocery shopping, keep your food preparation space safe from cross-contamination, or fill your pantry with gluten-free goodies.

I wrote this book to help you safely eat gluten-free all on your own. Read the first chapter to learn how to ask the right questions about eating gluten-free on your college campus, and how to communicate with your roommates, friends, and professors about your diet when the need arises. It also includes a quick review of what's gluten-free and what isn't so you can shop and cook for yourself. And the rest of the book? It's an awesome guide to making fast, easy, healthy, and delicious gluten-free meals that are perfect for college kids of any age!

It's college! Stay safe, eat well, and have a blast!

Sincerely,

Carrie S. Forbes

Welcome to the EVERYTHING® Series!

These handy, accessible books give you all you need to tackle a difficult project, gain a new hobby, comprehend a fascinating topic, prepare for an exam, or even brush up on something you learned back in school but have since forgotten.

You can choose to read an Everything® book from cover to cover or just pick out the information you want from our four useful boxes: e-questions, e-facts, e-alerts, and e-ssentials.

We give you everything you need to know on the subject, but throw in a lot of fun stuff along the way, too.

We now have more than 400 Everything® books in print, spanning such wide-ranging categories as weddings, pregnancy, cooking, music instruction, foreign language, crafts, pets, New Age, and so much more. When you're done reading them all, you can finally say you know Everything®!

QUESTION

Answers to
common questions

FACT

Important snippets
of information

ALERT

Urgent
warnings

ESSENTIAL

Quick
handy tips

PUBLISHER Karen Cooper

MANAGING EDITOR, EVERYTHING® SERIES Lisa Laing

COPY CHIEF Casey Ebert

ASSOCIATE PRODUCTION EDITOR Mary Beth Dolan

ACQUISITIONS EDITOR Lisa Laing

DEVELOPMENT EDITOR Eileen Mullan

EVERYTHING® SERIES COVER DESIGNER Erin Alexander

Visit the entire Everything® series at *www.everything.com*

THE
EVERYTHING®
GLUTEN-FREE
COLLEGE
COOKBOOK

Carrie S. Forbes

Avon, Massachusetts

An Everything® Series Book.
Everything® and everything.com® are registered trademarks of F+W Media, Inc.

Published by Adams Media, a division of F+W Media, Inc.
57 Littlefield Street, Avon, MA 02322. U.S.A.
www.adamsmedia.com

Contains material adapted and abridged from *The Everything® Healthy College Cookbook*
by Nicole Cormier, RD, copyright © 2010 by F+W Media, Inc., ISBN 10: 1-4405-0411-3, ISBN
13: 978-1-4405-0411-2; *The Everything® Gluten-Free Cookbook* by Rick Marx and Nancy T.
Maar, copyright © 2006 by F+W Media, Inc., ISBN 10: 1-59337-394-5, ISBN 13: 978-1-59337-394-
8; *The Everything® College Cookbook* by Rhonda Lauret Parkinson, copyright © 2005 by
F+W Media, Inc., ISBN 10: 1-59337-303-1, ISBN 13: 978-1-59337-303-0; *The Everything® Guide to
Living Gluten-Free* by Jeanine Friesen, copyright © 2013 by F+W Media, Inc., ISBN 10: 1-4405-
5184-7, ISBN 13: 978-1-4405-5184-0; *The Everything® Busy Mom's Cookbook* by Susan Whetzel,
copyright © 2013 by F+W Media, Inc., ISBN 10: 1-4405-5925-2, ISBN 13: 978-1-4405-5925-9-2;
The Everything® Paleolithic Diet Cookbook by Jodie Cohen and Gilaad Cohen, copyright ©
2011 by F+W Media, Inc., ISBN 10: 1-4405-1206-X, ISBN 13: 978-1-4405-1206-3.

ISBN 10: 1-4405-6568-6
ISBN 13: 978-1-4405-6568-7
eISBN 10: 1-4405-6569-4
eISBN 13: 978-1-4405-6569-4

Printed in the United States of America.

10   9   8   7   6   5   4   3   2   1

Always follow safety and common-sense cooking protocol while using kitchen utensils,
operating ovens and stoves, and handling uncooked food. If children are assisting in the
preparation of any recipe, they should always be supervised by an adult.

This book is available at quantity discounts for bulk purchases.
For information, please call 1-800-289-0963.

Contents

Introduction

SO YOU'RE HEADED TO college. You've packed your bags, signed up for your first classes, and purchased your textbooks. It's time to live on your own and be free. Except, you can't eat gluten. You may have celiac disease, gluten sensitivity, and/or food allergies, and it's up to you to figure out how you can eat safely now that you're away from home.

A few years ago, the term *gluten-free* seemed like a foreign language. Thankfully, huge strides have been made in the medical field, and more and more doctors are becoming better educated about celiac disease and the gluten-free diet. They are also much quicker to have their patients tested for a gluten-related allergy. With all of these changes occurring, it's no wonder that the gluten-free food market has exploded with products over the past few years. However, while there are now tons of resources available for children and adults, there's one group of people who are often left out: you, the college student.

College students seem to fall in that gray area between youth and adulthood, and in many ways, you're left on your own to swim the "shark (or gluten)-infested" waters of college living. Adults often have a hard time learning how to adapt to the gluten-free diet, and they have complete control over what they eat. But you? As a college student, you may have some control over your meals, especially if you are buying them yourself from the grocery store, but many colleges require students to purchase meal plans so that they will have access to "balanced" meals on campus. Unfortunately, not all college campuses are up to par when it comes to making safe, gluten-free meals.

The first chapter of this book will help you learn the right questions to ask when you are visiting college campuses. The experience of simply visiting colleges and their dining halls will help you "get a taste" of what life will be like on your own. As a gluten-free college student, one thing that's very important for you to learn is that you are your own best advocate. As a young adult, you are now responsible for your health and you have be able to take charge of your gluten-free diet. This means that you have to be willing to stand up for yourself and ask for help in figuring out the best ways to get safe meals on your college campus. There are people there to help you, and this book will assist you in finding the right staff members and asking the right questions.

College should be a really fun and exciting time for you. If you feel overwhelmed with trying to fully follow the gluten-free diet away from your "safe zone" of home, think about joining a local gluten-free support group, either in person or through social media sites like Facebook. Even if there aren't a lot of other people your age in the group, you will get to know other people who have been gluten-free for a long time and have a huge depth of knowledge about living gluten-free in general. Make it a priority to find other gluten-free students on campus and share your difficulties with them as well as your successes (like when you find a great gluten-free option).

Another great thing about college? If you haven't started before, now is a great time to learn how to cook and bake on your own. Preparing your own gluten-free meals is an important skill to learn, and college is a great time to do it. This cookbook provides you with 300 easy, healthy recipes and will encourage you to learn more about cooking your own gluten-free meals.

From ideas for easy, quick breakfasts, lunches, or late-night dinners to party foods and study grub, this book will teach you basic gluten-free cooking techniques and baking skills. You'll be able to make delicious gluten-free muffins, cookies, and brownies from scratch (or using your favorite gluten-free baking mix) that will impress any of your college friends. You'll also find vegetarian meals, stellar sandwiches, and a whole chapter of fast microwave meals. This book will give you everything you need to make the transition to gluten-free college life fun, easy, and delicious.

CHAPTER 1

The Gluten-Free College Experience

These days, more and more students are entering college with celiac disease, gluten sensitivity, and/or food allergies. It's currently estimated that one in 133 people have celiac disease, and even more may have non-celiac gluten sensitivity. This means college dining halls and cafes are slowly becoming more aware and educated about how to prepare gluten-free food for their students with dietary challenges. However, many colleges are still learning the gluten-free ropes. This chapter will review the basics of being gluten-free, as well as teach you how to navigate your college life as a gluten-free student.

What Is Gluten?

To begin, let's review what gluten is and where it's found. *Gluten* is the term used for several types of proteins found in wheat, barley, and rye. The proteins gliadin and glutelin are found in these grains and together form a substance called gluten. Gluten is a "storage protein," which means that it holds the key ingredients for these grains to continue proliferating. Gluten is primarily found in foods such as traditional breads, pasta, cakes, muffins, crackers, pizza, etc. These grains are used because gluten provides excellent elasticity, structure, and texture to baked goods. Gluten is what causes pizza to have a chewy, stretchy texture. Gluten gives French bread its soft, white center and chewy crust. Gluten makes cinnamon rolls stretchy, soft, and light. Gluten helps give structure to yeast as it expands bread dough so that the bread becomes tall when rising and stays tall after baking and cooling.

FACT

Did you know that there are no "typical" signs and symptoms of celiac disease according to the Mayo Clinic? Celiac patients of all ages, genders, and races often report a wide range of symptoms that can be anything from well-known signs, such as diarrhea, constipation, or malabsorption of nutrients, to migraine headaches, brain "fog," loss of memory, joint pain, irritability, depression, neuropathy, osteoporosis, and so on.

Gluten can be deceiving for several reasons. The biggest reason is that there are a number of foods and food products that contain gluten, but because gluten is simply a protein found in the ingredient itself, it's not listed on the package. By law, the top eight food allergens must be listed on every food label in the United States. This is helpful because wheat is one of the top eight allergens. The remaining seven are milk, eggs, tree nuts (cashews, almonds, walnuts, etc.), fish, shellfish, peanuts, and soy.

However, in addition to wheat, you also need to avoid these foods (most are derivatives of wheat), which also contain gluten:

- Barley
- Bulgar

- Couscous
- Durum flour
- Farina
- Graham flour
- Kamut
- Rye
- Seminola
- Spelt
- Triticale (a cross between rye and wheat)

As a matter of fact, it's often a good idea (especially when you first receive your diagnosis) to *only* eat foods that are either naturally gluten-free or listed as gluten-free until you have a better understanding of how to read food and nutrition labels.

Are You Sure That's Gluten-Free?

When you're deciding which college to go to, it will seem like there are a million things you need to consider. While maintaining a gluten-free diet shouldn't stop you from attending the school of your dreams, you will want to make sure you research your options and talk to as many people as you can at each college to learn if the school will be able to adequately accommodate your dietary needs.

The Dining Hall

One of the first things you will want to do when you're visiting colleges is scope out the dining hall. You will probably want to meet with the dining services manager, the school's dietician or nutritionist, and possibly even the director of housing or residential life. Ask some of following questions:

- Do you offer gluten-free options for students at every meal?
- Are the gluten-free meals prepared in a separate area? What steps do the dining-hall staff take to prevent cross-contamination?
- Are the dining-hall staff trained in food allergies and handling gluten-free food?

- Are you required to be on the school meal plan? Can you be on a partial meal plan if the school doesn't offer a wide selection of gluten-free choices?
- Does the dining hall offer full disclosure of all ingredients in the gluten-free foods offered? (For example, if serving barbecue chicken, would the dining hall list all the ingredients in the barbecue sauce so the student is certain the sauce is gluten-free or just say the chicken has barbecue sauce on it?)
- Is there a gluten-free support group on campus, or a place where gluten-free students hang out to chat? How can you connect with other gluten-free students?

If you're attending a large university, there may be several dining halls. You'll need to know if only one or all of the dining halls accommodate gluten-free students. If there is only one, can you be placed in a dorm nearby?

While you're visiting, have a meal in the dining hall. You will want to experience a gluten-free meal in person with your family. Doing this will give you a better idea of the time and effort the staff will take to give you a safe meal. Ask questions while you're ordering your food. See if your food is prepared on the same grill or preparation space as all of the other food. Check to make sure the server changes gloves to prepare your food. Were you only offered a salad or limited to the salad bar? This meal will give you an idea of the ease or difficulties you might have eating for the duration of your college career.

Preparing Your Own Meals

You will also want to prepare some meals in your dorm room or apartment, as well as eat out locally. Spend some time doing online research to find out which local grocery stores have gluten-free foods, along with which local restaurants have gluten-free menus. There are countless websites available now that can help you find local gluten-free resources, such as community and college support groups, gluten-free books to help educate yourself, free gluten-free recipes and menus, and even gluten-free shopping guides (see Appendix B). More and more college communities are building gluten-free bakeries and restaurants that offer gluten-free baked goods, such as pizza, sandwich bread, cakes, and cookies.

ALERT

Every time you visit a restaurant, make sure to assess the knowledge of the waitstaff and kitchen staff. Even if you had the opportunity before your meal to research the restaurant, each visit and each location can be different. Ask your server for a gluten-free menu. If he doesn't understand what gluten-free means, you might want to find another restaurant. If he does understand what gluten-free means, ask him about the steps taken in the kitchen area to prevent cross-contamination so that your meal will be safe. Never be afraid to ask specific questions; your health is important!

Don't Be Afraid to Ask Questions

One of the keys to gluten-free survival in college is making your needs known to those around you. Don't be afraid to ask for help, and learn to be kind but aggressive about your gluten-free needs. You are now your best and most important advocate for your health and for safe, gluten-free meals. When you are getting your meals in the dining hall, repeatedly mention that you are gluten-free, make sure to read the labels of the gluten-free foods provided, and watch how the foods are prepared. Introduce yourself to the dining-hall staff and pleasantly remind them to use clean gloves or a clean preparation space if you notice it's not being done properly.

ESSENTIAL

Some colleges advise students with celiac disease or gluten sensitivity to register with the school's disability services because the condition may be covered under Section 504 of the Rehabilitation Act of 1973. While celiac disease doesn't fall under this category at all schools, some schools will provide unique benefits, such as allowing gluten-free students to have specific kitchen appliances like toasters or George Foreman Grills to cook safe meals in their rooms.

Remember, while you do need to talk and have open communication with the dining-hall managers and school nutritionists, the people who matter most are those who will serve you on a day-to-day basis. Since your dietary needs will be more complicated than other students', make sure to treat the people who serve you with kindness and patience. You can develop great relationships with the staff members who know you and understand your needs. Before long, they will know who you are and already be prepared to make your gluten-free meal as soon as they see you.

The Basics of a Gluten-Free Diet

Following a basic gluten-free diet essentially means you're going to start eating fresh, natural, and basic foods. You will not only be following a gluten-free diet but a very nutritionally balanced and healthy diet. When you're at college it can be really easy to rely on gluten-free boxed foods like crackers and cookies. While those options are great for some occasions, it will be a much healthier option to choose from some of the naturally gluten-free foods listed in this section. It will also help you to avoid gaining the infamous freshman fifteen!

Naturally Gluten-Free Foods

Whether you've been gluten-free for a while or you are brand new to the diet, you should try to eat as many naturally gluten-free foods as you can. Foods that naturally do not contain gluten include:

- Fruits
- Vegetables
- Beans
- Plain rice
- Plain nuts and seeds
- Unseasoned, fresh meats
- Unseasoned, fresh chicken
- Unseasoned, fresh fish
- Milk, cheese, and plain yogurt
- Eggs

Most of these foods (except for the beans) are often located around the perimeter of your grocery store. One thing to remember is that most naturally gluten-free foods will not come in a bag or box. With the exception of canned fruits, vegetables, beans, and nuts, you can find these foods in their natural state in the produce section, the meat section, and the dairy and egg section.

Cheap and Healthy Gluten-Free Pantry Staples

When you're first diagnosed with celiac disease or gluten sensitivity, the thought of having to change your entire diet can be extremely overwhelming. You start to think, no more bread, pasta, pizza, doughnuts, etc. While this may have been true five years ago (at least as far as purchasing these items in a local grocery store or restaurant goes), the gluten-free food industry has come a long way. There are many, many companies that are now producing high-quality and readily available gluten-free products, such as sandwich breads, pastas, flours, cookies, doughnuts, and so on.

Naturally gluten-free foods you will want to keep on hand if you have room:

- Baking ingredients, such as baking powder, baking soda, salt, individual herbs and spices (not seasonings, which may contain gluten), oils, and sugar
- Canned and jarred foods, such as plain vegetables, beans, fruits, peanut butter (and other nut butters), jams, jellies, and honey
- Canned tuna and chicken
- Plain rice (white, brown, basmati, jasmine, Arborio, etc., as long as they do not have seasonings)
- Fresh and frozen fruits and vegetables of all types
- Fresh and frozen unseasoned meats, chicken, fish, eggs, cheese, nuts, and milk

Make sure to keep your gluten-free foods separate from your roommates' regular "gluten-filled" foods. One way to do this is to keep the items in large plastic storage bins. You can keep these bins under your bed or in a closet, and keep gluten-free pantry staples, utensils, bowls, plates, and even cleaning supplies like sponges in the large bins. You will want to discuss with your roommate why it's so important to keep your food and cooking tools separate and how the smallest amount of gluten, even a few crumbs on a counter, could potentially make you sick.

Are there gluten-free options for drinking when I'm hanging out with friends at a bar or a party?
Just remember, you have to be over the age of twenty-one in the United States (or over eighteen in Canada) to legally drink; otherwise, you may just want to skip this question. You do have gluten-free drinking options. There are quite a few beers on the market now that are gluten-free, some brands of which include Redbridge, New Planet, and Bard's Tale. Remember, any "regular" beer does contain gluten, so avoid them completely. Distilled liquor is generally gluten-free, and hard ciders are an option that's becoming more widely available. Please remember to always drink responsibly and never drive when drinking.

Buying Gluten-Free Foods

Buying gluten-free specialty items, such as packaged crackers, cake mixes, cookies, and breads, can be very expensive. Gluten-free foods are often marked up as much as 500 percent more than their traditional wheat-containing counterparts. For example, a loaf of regular bread may cost about $1.50 at the average store, while a (generally much smaller) loaf of gluten-free bread can easily cost over $6.00.

Because specialty gluten-free foods can be so expensive, it's often very cost-effective for college students to eat as many naturally gluten-free foods as they can. Buying fruits and vegetables that are in season can help with food costs, as can purchasing canned or frozen versions during the winter months.

Make It Yourself!

Another great way to save money and stay healthy on a gluten-free diet is to make some of your meals and snacks from scratch. This book contains 300 recipes for super quick and easy meals you can make right in your dorm room with the help of a few basic appliances! If your school allows it, some of the appliances you may want to have include:

- **Microfridge:** A small dorm-room-size refrigerator with a built-in microwave. If you can't find one, at least try to buy a small refrigerator and a microwave separately.
- **Microwave:** This will be a super helpful tool to heat water quickly and to make quick soups and single-serving meals. Be sure to clean your microwave on a regular basis and teach your roommates to cover any gluten-filled meals with a paper towel to prevent gluten from getting into the cracks and crevices of the appliance.
- **Pasta or Rice Cooker:** Another great option for quick meals. Some colleges don't allow students to have this appliance, as it can be a fire hazard if it remains plugged in after cooking.
- **Toaster:** Gluten-free toast can be a comforting and quick meal if you're in a hurry. If your college does not allow you to have a toaster in your dorm room, invest in Toast It reusable toaster bags that you can use in the dining hall. These bags are heat-resistant and allow you to toast gluten-free bread in a shared toaster. These are also great for traveling. One bag can be reused multiple times, so they are a safe (and fun) option for making gluten-free toast.
- **George Foreman Grill:** A small countertop grill that's perfect for making grilled chicken or hamburgers safely. Again, these appliances may not be allowed in your dorm room, so double-check with your school's policies before purchasing.

Preventing Cross-Contamination

A major challenge with the gluten-free diet, especially in college, is learning how to prevent cross-contamination in your dorm room or apartment kitchen. As you probably know, cross-contamination means accidentally allowing gluten to get in or on a gluten-free food. For those who have celiac disease (and often those who are gluten intolerant), the tiniest crumb of gluten coming into contact with their food will make them sick. Often, celiac patients will have severe gastrointestinal distress, which in turn can cause extreme stomach pains, severe bloating, diarrhea, vomiting, constipation, and headaches. For many with celiac disease, the physical symptoms of cross-contamination can last for days.

Methods of Prevention

There are many different methods you can use to prevent cross-contamination when you have roommates or family members who eat regular foods that contain gluten. The easiest method of preventing cross-contamination is to simply not buy any gluten-containing foods. However, your roommate would probably be pretty upset if she came home to find that all of her regular foods had been tossed out! When you're in college (unless you're lucky enough to have all gluten-free roommates), you will probably have to share your kitchen or your room with others who eat regular food. Therefore, it's incredibly important to learn how to keep your food and cooking tools safe.

FACT

In addition to meals, you will also need to make sure that all of your medications and/or beauty and hygiene products are gluten-free. Lots of medications and vitamins contain gluten as a binder or filler. Shampoo, conditioner, detangler, toothpaste, lip balm, lipstick, eyeliner, and even face and hand cream can contain gluten. You will have to do your research either online or by calling companies specifically to find out which products contain gluten and which products are safe. Scientifically, gluten cannot get through your skin into your blood stream, but if you are showering, bathing, or brushing your teeth, there is a slight possibility that gluten could still enter your mouth, so it's best to avoid any products that contain gluten.

First, make sure to use a separate cutting board from your roommate. You can keep a gluten-free cutting board in a safe drawer on one side of the kitchen or in your large plastic container in your dorm room and keep the gluten-containing cutting board in an opposite drawer. If you are preparing meals, such as lunches or breakfasts to take to eat between classes, always prepare the gluten-free meals first, either on a clean surface or the gluten-free cutting board.

It sounds silly, but you can also use a color-coded and/or sticker system to differentiate gluten-free foods from gluten-containing foods. By placing large stickers of the same color on safe foods, it will be very easy for your roommates to tell the difference between your gluten-free foods and their regular foods. Along with color-coding, if you are keeping all of your foods together on a shelf, teach your roommates to place gluten-free foods above gluten-containing foods. For example, if you have a shelf that contains regular baking ingredients, place all gluten-free baking ingredients on the shelf above the regular foods. This way, you are reducing the chance of a crumb or speck of flour falling onto the gluten-free food.

When cooking gluten-free meals, you do not necessarily have to use specific pans, as long as the pans have been thoroughly washed in hot, soapy water and do not have any stuck-on crumbs or residue that could contain gluten. If you are worried about old crumbs being stuck on a particularly old pan, you can cover the pan in heavy-duty aluminum foil to protect the gluten-free foods from getting contaminated. However, you will need to use a designated gluten-free toaster.

If you use wooden utensils, remember to use your own separately marked gluten-free spoons and spatulas. Gluten can get embedded in tiny grains of wooden and/or bamboo utensils and bowls and therefore cannot be used for gluten-free foods, unless they are brand new and will only used for gluten-free preparations.

For your refrigerator, buy separate condiments and label them using the color-coding system. Remember, if someone places a knife that touched regular bread in your gluten-free mayonnaise jar, it's been cross-contaminated and can no longer be considered gluten-free. Therefore, it's very important to keep a special gluten-free shelf in your refrigerator or (to keep it easy) just have your own small refrigerator altogether. Alternately, you can buy condiments that come in plastic squeeze jars so that they never come in contact with dirty knives or spoons.

Here are a few good points to remember in helping prevent cross-contamination:

- Keep separate cutting boards in designated areas.
- Prepare gluten-free foods and meals on a clean counter or cutting board before preparing gluten-containing foods.
- Use a color-coded and/or sticker system to distinguish gluten-free items from gluten-containing items.
- Make sure to wash all cooking pans thoroughly in hot, soapy water.
- If in doubt, use foil to cover baking pans to keep foods safe.
- Store gluten-free foods above gluten-containing foods in the pantry.
- Have a separate color-coded area for gluten-free condiments in the refrigerator.
- If you're concerned that gluten-free food has come in contact with gluten, stick with the old adage, "If in doubt, throw it out."

CHAPTER 2

Breakfast

Brown Rice Crepes

You can stuff these crepes with salsa, jack cheese, and sour cream, or you can stuff them with mashed fruit, such as strawberries—the possibilities are endless! For this recipe, you can use either brown rice flour or sorghum flour.

INGREDIENTS | MAKES 12 CREPES

2 eggs

1 cup milk or buttermilk

1 teaspoon salt, or to taste

1 cup brown rice flour (or sorghum flour)

2 teaspoons sugar (optional)

2 tablespoons butter, melted

Vegetable oil for frying crepes

Storing Crepes

To store crepes, simply put a bit of corn flour on sheets of waxed paper and stack the crepes individually. Then put the whole thing in a plastic bag and store in the refrigerator for up to three days.

1. Place the eggs, milk or buttermilk, and salt in your food processor and process until smooth.

2. With the motor on low, slowly add the flour and spoon in the sugar (if you are making sweet crepes). Scrape down the sides of the bowl often. Add the melted butter.

3. Heat oil in a nonstick pan over medium heat. Pour in 1 cup batter. Tilt the pan to spread the batter evenly over entire surface. Cook for 3–4 minutes, turning once. Repeat with remaining batter.

4. Place crepes on sheets of waxed paper that have been dusted with extra corn flour.

5. To store, place in a plastic bag in refrigerator or freezer.

Mushroom, Ham, and Cheese Crepes

This crepe is excellent for brunch, lunch, or a light supper. You can vary the herbs.

INGREDIENTS | MAKES 12 CREPES

2 cups mushrooms, brushed clean and chopped

2 tablespoons olive oil

6 sage leaves, shredded

Salt and pepper, to taste

½ cup ricotta cheese

1 egg, lightly beaten

12 Brown Rice Crepes (sugar omitted; see recipe in this chapter)

1 recipe Basic Cream Sauce (see sidebar)

½ cup Parmesan cheese

Basic Cream Sauce

This cream sauce is the basis for a lot of cooking. You will need 3 tablespoons unsalted butter, 3 tablespoons brown rice flour or sorghum flour, 2 cups milk or cream, warmed, and salt and pepper to taste. Melt the butter in a small saucepan over medium-low heat and stir in the flour. Sauté, stirring, for 4–5 minutes. Add the warm milk or cream, whisking constantly until thickened to desired consistency. Just before serving, add salt and pepper. Makes 2 cups of sauce.

1. In a frying pan over medium heat, sauté the mushrooms in oil until softened. Add the sage leaves and salt and pepper.

2. In a medium bowl, mix the cooked mushrooms with the ricotta and egg.

3. Preheat the oven to 350°F.

4. Lay out the crepes. Put a tablespoon of the mushroom filling on one side of each. Roll and put in a baking dish. Cover with cream sauce and sprinkle with Parmesan cheese.

5. Bake for 20 minutes, and serve hot.

Basic Pancakes

These pancakes are great with mashed fresh peaches, strawberries, and/or blueberries.

INGREDIENTS | MAKES 16 PANCAKES

½ cup milk

2 eggs

1½ tablespoons butter, melted

1 tablespoon baking powder

1 cup white rice flour or brown rice flour (or substitute sorghum flour or garbanzo bean flour)

Extra butter, for frying pancakes

Flour Substitutions

Try substituting another flour in this recipe, such as sorghum flour, millet flour, or garbanzo bean flour, for an excellent savory pancake. You have so many choices—it's fun to exercise them.

1. In the bowl of a food processor, process the milk, eggs, and butter together.

2. Slowly add the baking powder and flour.

3. Heat griddle pan or large frying pan to medium. Drop a teaspoon of butter on it and when the butter sizzles, start pouring on the batter to make pancakes about 2" in diameter.

4. When bubbles come to the top, turn the pancakes and continue to fry until golden brown (about 2–4 minutes per side).

5. Place on a plate in a warm oven to keep warm while you make the others.

Banana Nut Pancakes

This recipe calls for the banana to be mashed into the batter,
but if you prefer you could also slice it and place it on top of the pancakes.

INGREDIENTS | SERVES 4

1 medium banana

1 recipe Basic Pancakes batter (see recipe in this chapter)

Butter, for frying

1 cup coarsely chopped walnuts

1 cup heavy cream, whipped with 1 tablespoon sugar

1. Place the banana in a food processor and process until smooth.

2. In a large bowl, combine the mashed banana and the prepared batter.

3. Heat a pan or griddle over medium heat.

4. Add butter to the pan and pour the batter onto the pan ½ cup at a time. Sprinkle nuts on top of each pancake.

5. Turn when the pancakes begin to bubble on top (about 2–4 minutes). Flip them over and cook on the other side for 2–4 minutes.

6. Remove pancakes from the pan and place on a warm platter. Serve with freshly whipped cream.

Blueberry or Strawberry Pancakes

Fruit on or inside pancakes is classic, healthy, and delicious.

INGREDIENTS | MAKES 12 PANCAKES

½ pint blueberries or strawberries

1 tablespoon sugar

1 teaspoon orange zest

1 recipe Basic Pancakes batter (see recipe in this chapter)

Butter, for frying

Freezing Fruit in Its Prime

There's nothing like blueberries in January, and not the fruit that comes loaded with sugary syrup in a can. When fresh blueberries are available, just rinse a quart and dry on paper towels. Place the berries on a cookie sheet in the freezer for a half-hour and then put them in a plastic bag for future use.

1. In a medium bowl, combine the fruit, sugar, and orange zest. Mash with a potato masher or pestle.

2. Heat a griddle over medium heat. Drop a teaspoon of butter on it and when the butter sizzles, start pouring on the batter to make pancakes about 2" in diameter. Spoon some of the mashed berries on top.

3. Flip when bubbles rise to the top of the pancakes, and brown on the other side (about 2–4 minutes per side). You will get some caramelization from the sugar and fruit—it's delicious. Top with more berries and whipped cream.

Maple Cakes

This is a wonderful, quick supper for when you're busy studying.
Serve with bacon, sausages, or ham and eggs if you are really hungry.

INGREDIENTS | MAKES 12 MEDIUM-SIZE PANCAKES

2 cups white rice flour or brown rice flour

5 teaspoons baking powder

1 teaspoon salt

2 tablespoons pure maple syrup

2 cups milk

2 eggs

1 tablespoon butter, melted

1½ cups corn kernels (fresh or frozen)

Butter or oil, for the griddle

1. In a large bowl, combine the flour, baking powder, and salt. Mix well.

2. Slowly add the syrup, milk, eggs, and butter, whisking to keep it light. Fold in the corn.

3. Heat the frying pan or griddle to medium. Add butter or oil. Drop the cakes on the griddle using a ladle. Fry until little bubbles form on the tops of the cakes. Turn and fry on the reverse side until golden brown (about 2–4 minutes per side).

4. Serve with maple syrup, or fresh berries and whipped cream.

Sweet Pepper and Gorgonzola Omelet

Rich creamy Gorgonzola cheese melting into eggs—simply delicious!
A nonstick pan takes all of the guesswork out of making omelets like this one.

INGREDIENTS | SERVES 2

2 teaspoons unsalted butter

4 eggs, well beaten

2 ounces crumbled Gorgonzola cheese

1 roasted red pepper, cut into strips

Salt and red pepper flakes, to taste

Eggs

Eggs are a versatile, all-purpose protein. Omelets are easy to digest and great for finicky appetites. Various vegetables, cheeses, and herbs make perfect fillings for omelets. The more creative the combination, the more interesting the omelet.

1. Heat a 10" nonstick pan over medium-high heat. Melt the butter and swirl to coat.

2. Add the eggs and swirl to distribute evenly in pan.

3. Place the cheese and pepper strips on one side of the omelet. Season with salt and pepper flakes.

4. Cook until just set (about 3–5 minutes), when it has the consistency of custard (soft and creamy but not liquid or runny).

5. Flip the plain side over the side with the cheese and peppers. Cut in half and serve on a warmed plate.

Hard-Boiled Eggs

The trick is to start with cold water, and then remove the eggs from the burner as soon as the water reaches a rolling boil. This prevents your eggs from tasting rubbery.

INGREDIENTS | SERVES 1 OR 2

2 eggs, any size

1. Place the eggs in a saucepan and cover with cold water to at least ½" above the eggs. Cover the pot with the lid and bring to a rolling boil over high heat.

2. As soon as the water is boiling, remove from heat. Let the eggs stand in the hot water for 17–20 minutes.

3. Remove the eggs from the saucepan and place in a bowl filled with cold water for at least 2 minutes or until cool enough to handle. Peel off the shells. These will keep in the refrigerator for about one week.

Peeling Hard-Boiled Eggs

First, never cook an egg by letting it sit in boiling water for several minutes—this will make it much harder to peel. To peel the egg, crack both ends on the countertop and roll it in your hands to loosen the shell. Then remove the shell, starting with the larger end.

Soft-Boiled Eggs

These taste delicious sprinkled with salt and pepper and served with toast or a good crusty bread.

INGREDIENTS | SERVES 1 OR 2

2 eggs, any size

1. Fill a pot with enough cold water so that there will be at least ½" of water above the eggs. Bring the water to a rolling boil.

2. Place the eggs in the pot and cook for 3–5 minutes (depending on your own preference for soft-boiled eggs).

3. Remove the eggs from the pot and place in cold water until cool enough to handle. Peel off the shells. These will keep in the refrigerator for up to one week.

Basic Poached Egg

For best results, use the freshest eggs possible. To add extra flavor,
try poaching the eggs in milk or broth instead of water.

INGREDIENTS | SERVES 1

Pinch salt
1 egg, any size

1. In a medium-size saucepan, bring 3" of water to a boil. Add the salt to help the water boil faster.

2. While waiting for the water to boil, break the egg into a small bowl.

3. When the water reaches a boil, turn the heat down until it is just simmering. Gently slide the egg into the simmering water and cook for 3–5 minutes, depending on how firm you like the yolk.

4. Remove the egg with a slotted spoon, letting any excess water drain into the saucepan. Use the slotted spoon to gently push aside any "threads" from the egg white. Serve plain or on gluten-free toast.

Perfect Scrambled Eggs

The trick to making perfect scrambled eggs is an evenly heated frying pan
and eggs that are at room temperature before cooking.

INGREDIENTS | SERVES 1 OR 2

2 eggs

2 tablespoons milk

Salt and pepper, to taste

Paprika, to taste

2 tablespoons butter or margarine

1. Break the eggs into a small bowl. Add the milk, salt and pepper, and paprika. Beat the eggs until they are an even color throughout.

2. In a small frying pan, melt the butter or margarine over low heat. Increase heat to medium-low and add the eggs.

3. Cook the eggs, using a spatula to turn sections of the egg from time to time so that the uncooked egg on top flows underneath. Adjust the heat as needed. For best results, remove the scrambled eggs from the pan when they are firm but still a bit moist (about 6–8 minutes).

Savory Scrambled Eggs

For extra flavor, stir in 2 tablespoons of sweet salsa just before removing the scrambled eggs from the pan.

INGREDIENTS | SERVES 1 OR 2

2 eggs

2 tablespoons milk

Salt and pepper, to taste

10 capers

4 tablespoons butter or margarine, divided

½ tomato, chopped

1 green onion, chopped

1. Break the eggs into a small bowl. Add the milk, salt and pepper, and capers. Beat until the eggs are an even color throughout.

2. In a small frying pan, melt 2 tablespoons of the butter or margarine on low heat. Add the tomato and green onion. Cook until the tomato is tender but still firm (about 3–5 minutes). Remove from pan and set aside. Clean the pan.

3. Melt the remaining 2 tablespoons of butter or margarine in the pan on low heat. Turn up the heat to medium-low and add the eggs.

4. Cook the eggs, using a spatula to turn sections of the egg from time to time so that the uncooked egg on top flows underneath. Adjust the heat as needed to cook the eggs.

5. When the eggs are nearly cooked (about 6 minutes), return the tomato and green onion to the pan. Cook the scrambled eggs until they are firm but still a bit moist (about 2 more minutes).

Basic Cheese Omelet

*Not sure which cheese to use? Both Cheddar and Monterey jack cheese
combine nicely with the chili powder and salsa in this recipe.*

INGREDIENTS | SERVES 1

2 eggs

2 tablespoons milk

Salt and pepper, to taste

¼ teaspoon chili powder, or to taste

1 tablespoon butter or margarine

¼ cup grated cheese of your choice

Salsa (optional)

Omelet Origins

Contrary to popular opinion, the dish combining egg with seasonings and various filling ingredients did not originate in France. Instead, its origins probably date back to ancient times, when kookoo, a Persian dish consisting of fried egg and chopped fresh herbs, was first eaten.

1. In a small bowl, lightly beat the eggs with the milk. Stir in the salt and pepper and chili powder.

2. Melt the butter or margarine in a frying pan over low heat. Swirl the butter around to coat the pan entirely.

3. Pour the egg mixture into the pan. Cook over low heat. After the omelet has been cooking for 2–3 minutes, sprinkle the grated cheese over half of the omelet.

4. Tilt the pan occasionally or lift the edges of the omelet with a spatula so that the uncooked egg runs underneath.

5. When the omelet is cooked evenly throughout (about 3–4 minutes more), loosen the edges of the omelet with a spatula. Carefully slide the spatula underneath the omelet and fold it in half. Slide the omelet onto a plate. Garnish with salsa if desired.

Western Omelet

In a true Western omelet, the vegetables are added to the egg mixture before the egg is fried in the pan.

INGREDIENTS | SERVES 1 OR 2

3 large eggs

3 tablespoons milk

Salt and pepper, to taste

⅛ teaspoon paprika, or to taste

3 tablespoons diced ham

3 tablespoons diced onion

3 tablespoons diced green bell pepper

2 tablespoons butter or margarine

Ketchup (optional)

Fabulous Frittata

Like egg foo yung, an Italian frittata is a combination of an omelet and a pancake, filled with sautéed meat, cheese, or vegetables. Like the omelet, a frittata can be a hearty lunch or dinner, as well as a breakfast dish. When preparing a frittata, feel free to experiment with using different types of cheese, such as Swiss, Gruyère, or Emmental.

1. In a medium bowl, lightly beat the eggs with the milk. Stir in the salt and pepper and paprika.

2. Add in the ham, onion, and green pepper and mix well.

3. Melt the butter or margarine in a frying pan over low heat. Swirl the butter around to coat the pan entirely.

4. Pour the egg mixture into the pan. Cook over low heat. After the omelet has been cooking for 2–3 minutes, tilt the pan occasionally or lift the edges of the omelet with a spatula so that the uncooked egg runs underneath.

5. When the omelet is cooked evenly throughout (about 3–4 minutes more), loosen the edges of the omelet with a spatula. Carefully slide the spatula underneath the omelet and fold it in half. If desired, fold two more times so that it forms a triangular shape. Slide the omelet onto a plate. Serve with ketchup, if desired.

Spinach and Ricotta Mini Quiches

*Who says quiche is just for old ladies? Try these delicious mini quiches
for over-the-top-taste in an easy-to-handle package!*

INGREDIENTS | SERVES 5

10 ounces chopped frozen spinach

2 eggs

1 cup skim ricotta cheese

1 cup low-fat shredded mozzarella cheese

1. Preheat the oven to 350°F. Place cupcake liners in a 12-hole muffin tin.

2. Heat the spinach in the microwave according to package directions or until soft and warm.

3. In a large bowl, beat the eggs. Add the spinach and blend together. Fold in the ricotta and shredded mozzarella cheese.

4. Fill each cup with egg-spinach mixture, about half way per cup. Bake for 30–35 minutes.

Very Veggie Omelet

*Change up this recipe by chopping up any vegetable you like
and adding it or substituting it for the peppers.*

INGREDIENTS | SERVES 2

4 large egg whites

1 large whole egg

¼ teaspoon salt

½ cup chopped red bell peppers

½ cup chopped green bell peppers

¼ cup chopped onions

½ cup chopped mushrooms

1 tablespoon olive oil

1. In a medium bowl, beat the egg whites and egg. Mix in the salt.

2. In a separate bowl, mix the red peppers, green peppers, onions, and mushrooms together.

3. Heat the olive oil in a small frying pan on low heat.

4. Pour in the egg mixture to coat the surface. Cook until edges show firmness (about 2–3 minutes).

5. Add the vegetable mixture so that it covers the entire egg mixture evenly. Fold one side over the other.

6. Flip the half-moon omelet so both sides are evenly cooked (about 2–3 more minutes per side).

Oven-Roasted Tomatoes

This is an excellent side dish to accompany eggs. The tomatoes pick up the flavors of any herbs used with them, and you can also add butter, cheese, and spices for extra flavor.

INGREDIENTS | SERVES 1

1 large red, ripe, and juicy tomato

1 teaspoon olive oil

1 teaspoon of your favorite herbs (rosemary, parsley, thyme, or basil)

Salt and pepper, to taste

1. Preheat the oven to 375°F.

2. Cut the tomato in half, from top to bottom. Use a melon baller to remove seeds. Sprinkle with oil, herbs, and salt and pepper.

3. Individually nest the tomato halves in aluminum foil, leaving the top open. Place open-end up directly on the rack in the oven. Roast for 15 minutes.

Peach Yogurt Smoothie

Can't find fresh peaches? You can use frozen peaches in this for a shortcut and a sherbet-like texture. The combination of yogurt and fruit will give your day a delicious boost.

INGREDIENTS | SERVES 2

½ banana

1½ cups cubed peaches

1 cup vanilla yogurt

¼ cup orange juice

1 teaspoon honey

1. Place all the ingredients in a blender and blend until smooth.

2. Pour into two glasses and serve as a quick breakfast for you and a friend, or refrigerate one serving and take the other in a travel mug on the go.

Creamy Carrot Smoothie

Yes, it sounds odd, but college is all about trying new things! The fruit juices will sweeten this smoothie, so you'll have all the benefits of carrot while still enjoying a tasty treat.

INGREDIENTS | SERVES 1

5 large carrots
1 tablespoon lemon juice
¼ cup orange juice
½ cup nonfat yogurt
½ cup skim milk

The Lowdown on Carrots

Loaded with beta-carotene, which is essential for healthy eyes, skin, and cell respiration, carrots are a nutritious superfood that's cheap and available year-round. Always choose fresh carrots that are crisp and tight-skinned, not limp, marred, or covered in brown blemishes.

1. In a blender or food processor grate the carrots. Separate the grated carrot from the juice using a fine strainer. Reserve the juice.

2. Place the grated carrot, lemon juice, orange juice, yogurt, and skim milk in a blender and blend until smooth.

3. Blend in the reserved carrot juice. Pour into a tall glass.

Raspberry Almond Milk Frappé

You can substitute maple syrup for the honey in this recipe for a different flavor, or substitute other flavors of frozen yogurt to add variety.

INGREDIENTS | SERVES 2

1 cup frozen raspberries
¾ cup vanilla frozen yogurt
½ cup almond milk
⅛ teaspoon almond extract
1 teaspoon honey

1. Place all the ingredients in a blender and blend until smooth.

2. Pour into two glasses and serve as a quick breakfast.

Crunchy Creamy Yogurt Parfait

Yogurt parfaits are traditionally a healthy choice, and they're easy to make at home in no time at all. Mix and match different gluten-free cereals, yogurt flavors, and fruits for more delicious combinations.

INGREDIENTS | SERVES 1

2 tablespoons gluten-free Rice Chex cereal, crushed

4 ounces sugar-free vanilla yogurt

¼ cup sliced strawberries

Layer the ingredients in a tall travel cup, starting with the Rice Chex, then the yogurt, and finally the strawberries.

Breakfast Fruit Salad

Mandarin oranges are a citrus fruit that looks more flat like a tangerine than round like an orange. They're high in vitamin C. When buying canned mandarins, always choose the ones without the heavy syrup.

INGREDIENTS | SERVES 4

2 cups cubed Gala or Braeburn apples

1½ cups cubed pears

1 cup mandarin orange slices

½ cup sliced kiwi

¼ cup fresh blueberries

1 tablespoon dried cranberries

3 tablespoons sunflower seeds

Combine all the ingredients in a large bowl. Put one serving in a container to take with you and refrigerate the leftovers.

Dried Fruits and Nuts

Dried fruits and nuts are the perfect foods for college students to have on hand. They make quick, healthy snacks and they can be thrown into all sorts of recipes, from trail mixes to salads. Also, if properly stored, they can stay fresh for a long time, which means you'll always have some ready when you need them.

Blackberry Apple Smoothie

When berries are not in season, frozen berries will work just as well. Frozen berries can also add a nice texture to a berry smoothie. Test the texture as you blend to get the perfect fruity, crunchy consistency.

INGREDIENTS | SERVES 1

1 cup blackberries
1 apple, sliced
1 cup nonfat yogurt
½ cup skim milk

Combine all the ingredients in a blender until smooth. Pour into a tall glass.

Fruit Medley Smoothie

This smoothie is a great option if you're looking to boost your antioxidants.

INGREDIENTS | SERVES 1

¼ cup blueberries
¼ cup fresh strawberries
1 large peach, sliced
1 cup raspberries
½ cup nonfat yogurt
½ cup skim milk

Combine all the ingredients in a blender until smooth. Pour into a tall glass.

Have a Fruit Frenzy

This isn't called a medley smoothie for nothing. Experiment with all different kinds of fruit in this recipe, from mango to pineapple to kiwi. Chances are, most combos will taste great. Oh, and make sure you keep the seeds in fruits like raspberries and kiwi. They contain an extra dose of fiber.

Breakfast Burrito

Burritos are favorites for lunch and dinner. Why not try a breakfast variation? Make sure to read the ingredients on the corn tortillas package to be certain they are gluten-free, as some brands contain wheat flour.

INGREDIENTS | SERVES 1

1 teaspoon oil
1 large egg, beaten
1 (6") corn tortilla
1 tablespoon shredded Cheddar cheese
1½ teaspoons salsa

My Corn Tortilla Won't Bend

Corn tortillas stored in the fridge have a tendency to break if used cold. To make them roll nicely, either microwave between two damp paper towels for 30 seconds, or fry them for 1 minute per side in a lightly oiled pan over medium-high heat.

1. Heat oil in a small frying pan over medium heat. Add the egg and stir it while it is cooking to scramble it. Once the egg is no longer wet, it is done (about 6–8 minutes).

2. Place the scrambled egg in the center of the tortilla. Top with cheese and salsa. Roll up and eat.

3. If you want your cheese melted, you can heat the burrito with cheese in the microwave for about 15 seconds before topping with the salsa.

Buttermilk Pancakes

If you do not have any buttermilk on hand, you can use milk or nondairy milk instead.
Just add 1 tablespoon of lemon juice to the milk, stir, and let sit for five minutes before using.

INGREDIENTS | SERVES 5

1 cup brown rice flour

⅓ cup, plus 2 tablespoons, arrowroot starch or tapioca starch

½ teaspoon xanthan gum

1½ teaspoons baking powder

½ teaspoon baking soda

½ teaspoon salt

1¾ cups buttermilk

¼ cup oil

2 large eggs

1 teaspoon vanilla extract

1. In a large mixing bowl, whisk together the brown rice flour, arrowroot starch, xanthan gum, baking powder, baking soda, and salt until evenly mixed.

2. In a smaller mixing bowl, whisk together the buttermilk, oil, eggs, and vanilla.

3. Pour the wet ingredients into the dry ingredients, and stir until just mixed. It is all right if the batter still appears slightly lumpy.

4. Pour ½ cup batter onto a lightly greased frying pan or griddle over medium-high heat, making pancakes that are about 4"–5" in diameter.

5. Flip the pancakes over once bubbles form on the top of the pancakes. Cook until second side is golden brown. If the pancake is browning too fast, reduce the heat.

6. Repeat with the remaining batter.

Baked Pumpkin Crunch Oatmeal

Baked oatmeal is so easy to put together, smells amazing while baking, and makes a great breakfast—even on the mornings when you are short on time. It can also be baked ahead of time and simply reheated for a warm, satisfying breakfast.

INGREDIENTS | SERVES 9

½ cup pumpkin purée (not pie filling)

1 large egg

⅓ cup maple syrup

1 teaspoon vanilla extract

⅔ cup milk

1 teaspoon ground cinnamon

½ teaspoon ground ginger

¼ teaspoon fresh ground nutmeg

½ teaspoon salt

2 cups certified gluten-free oats

1½ teaspoons baking powder

½ cup chopped pecans (optional)

1. Preheat oven to 350°F. Lightly grease an 8" × 8" square baking pan. Set aside.

2. In a large bowl, combine all the ingredients.

3. Pour into lightly greased baking pan and bake in preheated oven for 30–35 minutes. Let oatmeal sit for 5 minutes before serving. Topped with some ice cream or whipped cream, Baked Pumpkin Crunch Oatmeal also makes a great dessert.

Reasons to Eat Your (Gluten-Free) Oats

Not only does baked oatmeal taste great, it's also good for you! Oats help lower cholesterol, regulate blood sugar, are a great source of iron, and help keep you full for hours.

Cinnamon-Raisin French Toast

In no time at all you can have warm, delicious French toast,
the perfect meal to get you fueled up for a day of classes.

INGREDIENTS | SERVES 4

2 large eggs

⅓ cup milk

2 tablespoons butter, divided

8 slices gluten-free raisin bread or gluten-free whole-grain bread (such as Udi's Whole Grain)

Syrup (optional)

Confectioners' sugar (optional)

1. In a pie plate or large bowl, beat the eggs and milk with a whisk.

2. In a large frying pan, melt 1 tablespoon of the butter over medium heat.

3. Dip the slices of bread in the egg mixture, coating both sides.

4. Put 2–4 slices of bread into the heated frying pan at a time and cook 1–2 minutes on each side until golden brown. Continue with remaining butter and slices of bread.

5. Serve with your favorite syrup or sprinkled with confectioners' sugar.

Fluffy Waffles

Waffles are a versatile meal that can be eaten any time of day,
and are perfect for a quick snack on the run.

INGREDIENTS | SERVES 5

1⅓ cups brown rice flour

¾ cup arrowroot starch or tapioca starch

1 teaspoon xanthan gum

2 teaspoons baking powder

1 teaspoon baking soda

½ teaspoon salt

2 teaspoons granulated sugar

2 cups buttermilk

6 tablespoons oil

2 teaspoons vanilla extract

2 large eggs

Feeding a Crowd

To serve the whole family a delicious meal of waffles at the same time, you can keep the waffles hot and crisp by placing them in a 250°F oven until ready to serve.

1. Lightly oil your waffle iron and set to desired temperature. Allow to preheat while you prepare the batter.

2. In a large mixing bowl, whisk together the brown rice flour, arrowroot starch or tapioca starch, xanthan gum, baking powder, baking soda, salt, and sugar.

3. In a small mixing bowl, whisk together the buttermilk, oil, vanilla, and eggs.

4. Pour the wet ingredients into the dry ingredients and stir until just mixed.

5. Cook on preheated waffle iron according to manufacturer's instructions.

Lemon Poppy Seed Muffins

Although the glaze is optional, it really enhances the tangy citrus flavor of the muffins.

INGREDIENTS | SERVES 12

⅔ cup sugar

Zest of 1 large lemon (or 2 small ones)

1 cup sorghum flour

½ cup brown rice flour

¼ cup tapioca starch

1 teaspoon xanthan gum

2 teaspoons baking powder

1 teaspoon baking soda

½ teaspoon salt

Juice of 1 large lemon (or 2 small) plus enough milk to make 1 cup

2 large eggs

1 teaspoon vanilla extract

½ cup (1 stick) butter, melted and cooled

2 tablespoons poppy seeds

½ cup sugar

¼ cup lemon juice

1. Grease a 12-cup muffin tin or line with paper liners. Preheat the oven to 375°F.

2. In a large bowl, use your hands to rub together the ⅔ cup sugar and the lemon zest until the sugar is damp and the mixture smells like lemon. Add the sorghum flour, brown rice flour, tapioca starch, xanthan gum, baking powder, baking soda, and salt. Whisk until evenly combined.

3. In a separate bowl, whisk together the lemon juice plus enough milk to make 1 cup, eggs, vanilla, and melted butter.

4. Pour the wet ingredients into the dry ingredients and mix until just combined. Stir in the poppy seeds.

5. Spoon the mixture into the prepared muffin tin. Bake in preheated oven for 18–20 minutes or until golden brown and they spring back when gently touched.

6. While the muffins are baking, prepare the lemon glaze. In a small saucepan over medium-high heat, combine the ½ cup sugar and ¼ cup lemon juice. Stir until it comes to a boil. Boil for 30 seconds before removing from heat. Set aside until the muffins are done.

7. Remove muffins from the oven and allow to sit for 5 minutes before removing from the muffin tin to a wire cooling rack. While the muffins are still warm, either brush the tops with the glaze, or dip the tops in the glaze. Allow to cool completely before storing in an airtight container.

Best Banana-Berry Smoothie

You can enjoy this smoothie any time of year. It's delicious, refreshing, and good for you. And it's a great choice for breakfast on the go!

INGREDIENTS | SERVES 2

1 frozen banana

½ cup frozen berries (raspberries, blueberries, strawberries, or any combination you choose)

1 (8-ounce) container vanilla yogurt

½ cup milk

1. Put all the ingredients into a blender.

2. Put the lid on and blend for 1 minute or until smooth. Pour into two large glasses and enjoy.

Freezing a Banana

When a banana becomes too ripe and soft to eat, you can freeze it to keep on hand for smoothies and frozen beverages. Peel the banana and then wrap it up in plastic wrap and place it in the freezer; otherwise, you will have a hard time removing the peel.

Corn Bread Muffins

These muffins are perfect served with a piping-hot bowl of chili, or eaten as a sweet treat topped with some fresh honey. To save a little time, feel free to use ¼ cup plus 1 tablespoon of your favorite gluten-free baking mix, such as Gluten-Free Bisquick, in place of the brown rice flour, arrowroot starch or tapioca starch, xanthan gum, baking soda, and salt.

INGREDIENTS | SERVES 12

½ cup (1 stick) butter or margarine

⅔ cup sugar (or ⅓ cup if you prefer less-sweet muffins)

2 large eggs

1 cup buttermilk

½ teaspoon baking soda

1 cup gluten-free cornmeal such as Bob's Red Mill

⅔ cup brown rice flour

¼ cup plus 1 tablespoon arrowroot starch or tapioca starch

½ teaspoon xanthan gum

½ teaspoon salt

1. Preheat oven to 350°F. Lightly grease a muffin pan and set aside.

2. In a large microwave-safe bowl, melt the butter or margarine.

3. Stir the sugar into the melted butter. Add eggs and stir to combine. Stir in buttermilk.

4. In a medium-size mixing bowl, whisk together the baking soda, cornmeal, brown rice flour, arrowroot starch or tapioca starch, xanthan gum, and salt. Add to the wet ingredients and stir until few lumps remain.

5. Scoop batter into prepared muffin tin.

6. Bake in preheated oven for 20 minutes or until a toothpick inserted into the center comes out clean.

7. Allow to cool in the muffin pan for 5 minutes before removing to cooling rack. Best served warm.

Banana Chocolate Chip Scones

These scones are perfect as is, or topped with some cream cheese or chocolate hazelnut spread. Just like Corn Bread Muffins (see this chapter), feel free to use 1½ cups of your favorite gluten-free baking mix, such as Gluten-Free Bisquick, in place of the brown rice flour, tapioca starch, xanthan gum, baking powder, baking soda, and salt to save a little time.

INGREDIENTS | SERVES 8

1¼ cups brown rice flour, plus some for baking sheet

¼ cup arrowroot starch or tapioca starch

4 teaspoons xanthan gum

2 teaspoons baking powder

1 teaspoon baking soda

½ teaspoon salt

¼ cup sugar

6 tablespoons cold butter, cut into chunks

1 egg yolk

1 small ripe banana, mashed (about ⅓ cup)

½ cup sour cream or plain yogurt

1 teaspoon vanilla extract

½ cup gluten-free mini chocolate chips

1 egg white, beaten (for brushing)

1. Preheat the oven to 400°F. Line a baking sheet with parchment paper and sprinkle with some brown rice flour. Set aside.

2. Place the brown rice flour, tapioca starch, xanthan gum, baking powder, baking soda, salt, and sugar in the bowl of a food processor. Pulse to mix the ingredients.

3. Add the cold butter and pulse until the mixture forms pea-size chunks.

4. Add the egg yolk, mashed banana, sour cream or plain yogurt, vanilla extract, and mini chocolate chips. Pulse again until the dough just comes together in a ball. Spoon the dough onto your parchment-lined baking sheet.

5. Dusting your hands with brown rice flour, quickly form the dough into a disk, about 10" round and ¾"–1" thick. Cut into eight even wedges and move the wedges apart so they are not touching each other. This will allow them to bake evenly.

6. Brush the tops of the scones with the egg white.

7. Bake in preheated oven for 18–20 minutes or until the tops are a nice golden brown. Remove from oven and move scones to wire cooling rack for 15 minutes before serving.

8. Store in an airtight container once the scones are completely cool.

Breakfast Salad

Salads aren't just for lunch and dinner anymore—they can be round-the-clock meals.
Not only are they easy to prepare, you can make endless combinations so you never get bored!

INGREDIENTS | SERVES 1

3 cups baby spinach leaves

4 large eggs, hard-boiled, peeled, and quartered

2 slices bacon, cooked and chopped

½ cup sliced cucumber

½ avocado, diced

½ apple, sliced

Juice of ½ lemon

1. Arrange the spinach leaves on a plate and top with the eggs and bacon.

2. Add the cucumber, avocado, and apple to top of salad.

3. Squeeze fresh lemon juice over the salad. Serve immediately.

Mini Quiches

These are a tasty treat for breakfast or as perfect party apps, and they can be made in bulk.

INGREDIENTS | SERVES 8

6 large eggs

6 slices bacon

Cooking spray

½ cup chopped broccoli

½ cup sliced mushrooms

½ cup diced onions

½ cup diced red bell pepper

1. Preheat oven to 325°F. Line a muffin tin with eight foil cups.

2. In a medium bowl, whisk the 6 eggs and set aside.

3. In a frying pan over medium heat, cook the bacon until crisp. Drain it on paper towels and chop into ½" pieces.

4. Spray a medium frying pan with cooking spray. Sauté the broccoli, mushrooms, onions, and red peppers for 5 minutes.

5. Pour the beaten eggs into the foil cups, filling each ⅔ of the way.

6. Add bacon and vegetables to each cup.

7. Bake for 25 minutes or until golden brown.

Egg Muffins

These are great to make in advance and take on the go.
They are also quite tasty with some sliced avocado.

INGREDIENTS | SERVES 18

2 tablespoons olive oil
12 large eggs
2 medium zucchini
1 bell pepper
1 green onion (optional)
3 cups fresh spinach
1 cup diced cooked ham

1. Preheat the oven to 350°F.

2. Grease two muffin pans with olive oil.

3. In a large bowl, whisk eggs well.

4. In a food processor, process the zucchini, pepper, and green onion (if using) until finely chopped but not smooth. If you do not own a food processor, simply use a sharp knife to cut all vegetables into very small, diced pieces.

5. Add the chopped vegetables to the eggs.

6. Finely chop the spinach with a sharp knife or in the food processor and add to the egg mixture.

7. Stir in the ham and mix well.

8. Fill each cup of the muffin pans halfway with the egg mixture.

9. Bake for 20–25 minutes or until the eggs are set in the middle.

Old-Fashioned Sweet Potato Hash Browns

*These sweet potato hash browns are likely to become one of your favorites.
They are easy to make and packed with flavor you will love!*

INGREDIENTS | SERVES 6

3 tablespoons coconut oil

3 medium sweet potatoes, peeled and grated

1 tablespoon cinnamon

1. Heat the coconut oil in large frying pan over medium-high heat.

2. Cook sweet potatoes in hot oil for 7 minutes, stirring often.

3. Once brown, sprinkle with cinnamon and serve.

CHAPTER 3

Lunch

Rhode Island Clam Chowder

This recipe is very traditional. Many cooks now substitute bacon for salt pork,
but it's better to make it the traditional way.

INGREDIENTS | SERVES 4

2 dozen cherrystone clams (2" wide)

3 ounces salt pork, chopped finely

1 large onion, chopped

1 carrot, peeled and chopped

2 stalks celery with tops, finely chopped

2 large Idaho potatoes, peeled and chopped

1 tablespoon cornstarch (more if you like it really thick)

2 bay leaves

1 teaspoon dried thyme

1 teaspoon celery salt

1 tablespoon Worcestershire sauce

3 cups clam broth

Freshly ground black pepper, to taste

½ cup chopped fresh parsley, for garnish

Is That Clam Alive or Dead?

Never eat a dead clam. Always run them under cold water and scrub vigorously with a brush. To test for life, tap two clams together. You should hear a sharp click, not a hollow thud. If the clam sounds hollow, tap it again, and then, if still hollow-sounding, discard it.

1. Scrub the clams and place them in a large pot. Add 2 cups water, cover the pot, and boil until the clams open. Remove the clams to a large bowl and let cool; reserve the liquid. Once cool, remove the clams, discard the shells, and chop the clams in a food processor.

2. In a soup pot, fry the salt pork until crisp. Drain on paper towels.

3. Add the vegetables to the pot and sauté until soft, about 10 minutes over medium heat. Blend in the cornstarch and cook for 2 more minutes, stirring.

4. Add the reserved liquid, bay leaves, thyme, and celery salt to the pot. Stir in the Worcestershire sauce, clam broth, the chopped clams, and the salt pork. Cover and simmer for ½ hour.

5. Before serving, remove bay leaf. Add black pepper to taste, garnish with chopped fresh parsley, and serve hot.

New England Clam Chowder

*With the base for Rhode Island Clam Chowder, you simply add cream
and/or milk to transform a clear chowder into a rich and creamy one.*

INGREDIENTS | SERVES 4–6

1 recipe Rhode Island Clam Chowder
(see recipe in this chapter), plus an extra
tablespoon cornstarch for a thicker
consistency
1 cup whole milk
1 cup cream
Parsley, chopped, for garnish

1. Bring the chowder base to a slow boil. Then add the milk and cream.

2. Reduce the heat to simmer and cover to let the ingredients marry. After you add the milk and cream, do not boil. If you do, your soup is likely to curdle. Taste and adjust seasonings if necessary. Garnish with freshly chopped parsley.

Manhattan Red Clam Chowder

*You can transform Rhode Island Clam Chowder to Manhattan with
the addition of some tomatoes. This is so easy and good.*

INGREDIENTS | SERVES 6

1 recipe Rhode Island Clam Chowder
(see recipe in this chapter)
1 (28-ounce) can chopped tomatoes with
their juice
Parsley, chopped, for garnish

After you have completed the recipe for Rhode Island Clam Chowder, add the tomatoes. Cover and simmer for 30 minutes. Serve hot. Garnish with chopped parsley.

Tomato or Cream in Your Clam Chowder?

Manhattan clam chowder, made with tomatoes, is a latecomer to the chowder arena. During the eighteenth and nineteenth centuries, tomato-based chowder was banned in New England. In fact, tomatoes were suspect for many years—it was the invention and distribution of ketchup in the early twentieth century that brought the tomato into its own in America.

Italian Sausage, Bean, and Vegetable Soup

There's nothing like a bowl of good soup, especially when you are in a hurry. This one is quickly made and will make you feel warm inside. When making this dish, keep in mind that you do need to check the label on any type of broth or stock, as some brands are thickened with wheat starch.

INGREDIENTS | SERVES 4–6

1 pound Italian sausage, either sweet or hot, cut into 1" pieces

1 large red onion, chopped

4 cloves garlic, minced

¼ cup olive oil

1 (28-ounce) can crushed tomatoes with their juice

1 bunch escarole, washed, base stems removed, chopped

2 (13-ounce) cans gluten-free beef broth (check to make sure wheat starch is not present)

2 (13-ounce) cans white beans

1 tablespoon dried oregano

1 cup grated Parmesan cheese

1. In a frying pan over medium heat, sauté the sausage, onion, and garlic in the olive oil. When the onion and garlic are soft, add the rest of the ingredients, except the Parmesan cheese.

2. Cover and simmer over very low heat for 30 minutes. Garnish with Parmesan cheese and serve.

Thick and Rich Cream of Broccoli Soup

This soup can be served in gluten-free bread bowls as a hearty lunch or supper. Garnish with a few small shrimp floated on the top.

INGREDIENTS | SERVES 4–6

1 pound broccoli

1 tablespoon olive oil or butter

1 large sweet onion, chopped

2 cloves garlic, chopped

2 tablespoons cornstarch dissolved in ⅓ cup cold water

3 cups low-salt, gluten-free chicken broth

½ cup dry white wine

¼ teaspoon freshly grated nutmeg

Juice and rind of 1 lemon

Salt and freshly ground pepper, to taste

1 cup heavy cream

¾ cup minced prosciutto or other smoked ham

1. Wash, trim, and coarsely chop the broccoli. Set it aside in a colander to drain.

2. In a large soup pot, heat the oil or butter and add the onion and garlic. Sauté until softened.

3. Stir in the cornstarch-water mixture and other liquid ingredients. Mix in the broccoli, nutmeg, juice and rind of lemon, and salt and pepper.

4. Simmer the soup, covered, until the broccoli is tender, about 15 minutes. Remove the lemon rind.

5. Move to a blender and purée in batches.

6. Return to the pot and stir in the cream and ham. Reheat but do not boil. Serve hot.

Adding Depth of Flavor to Soup

Adding sausage, ham, or bacon to a soup enriches the flavor of soup. The salt and smoke used in the pork-curing process, and the herbs and spices used in sausage, also add to the flavor of a soup or stew. Smoked ham hocks are a classic tasty touch in Southern cooking. They are inexpensive and meaty, but the skin and bones must be removed before the soup is served.

Fresh Spring Soup with Baby Peas

Garnish this soup with a few cooked shrimp or a few tablespoons smoked ham, finely chopped.

INGREDIENTS | SERVES 4

1 cup chopped spring onions or scallions

2 cloves garlic, smashed

2 cups baby spinach

10 young dandelion greens (small leaves only) or arugula leaves

¼ cup olive oil

2 ounces cornstarch

3 cups gluten-free vegetable stock

⅛ teaspoon ground allspice

Zest of ½ lemon, minced

1½ cups fresh baby peas or 1 (10-ounce) package frozen peas

1 cup heavy cream

Salt and pepper, to taste

1. In a stockpot over medium heat, sauté the onions or scallions, garlic, and greens in olive oil for 5 minutes, to wilt them.

2. Whisk in the cornstarch and vegetable stock. Stir in the allspice and lemon zest. When smooth, move to a blender and purée.

3. Return the soup to the pot and add the peas. Cook for 5–8 minutes or until tender.

4. Add the cream and salt and pepper. Do not boil, but serve hot.

Springtime, Anytime!

You can enjoy spring flavors any time of year, thanks to California herbs and frozen petit pois (tiny peas). If you can get spring onions, fine; if not, use scallions.

Summer Cucumber Soup

This is so refreshing on a hot day. With only a few ingredients, you can make a delicious summer soup.

INGREDIENTS | SERVES 4

2 English cucumbers, peeled and chopped

2 cups buttermilk

1 cup sour cream

2 teaspoons salt

Juice of 1 lemon

Rind of ½ lemon

⅔ tablespoon snipped fresh dill weed (snipped to ¼")

½ cup snipped fresh chives (snipped to ¼")

Freshly ground pepper, to taste

Mix all the ingredients in a nonreactive ceramic or porcelain bowl. Chill overnight. Serve in chilled bowls.

Yellow Squash and Apple Soup

This is a refreshing summer soup with loads of flavor.
Make a lot and serve it the next day to beat the heat.

INGREDIENTS | SERVES 4

2 shallots, minced

1 Granny Smith apple, peeled, cored, and chopped

2 medium yellow squash, chopped

4 tablespoons butter

3 cups fresh orange juice

1 cup apple juice

Juice of 1 fresh lime

¼ teaspoon ground cumin

⅛ teaspoon ground nutmeg

Salt and freshly ground white pepper, to taste

4 tablespoons sour cream, for garnish

1. In a large pot, sauté the shallots, apples, and squash in the butter until tender.

2. Add the rest of the ingredients except the sour cream. Stir to combine.

3. Move the soup to a blender and purée in batches.

4. Return the soup to the pot and bring it to a boil. Serve it hot or cold, garnished with sour cream.

Middle Eastern Hummus

This is a great, healthy snack to munch on while studying. Hummus makes a nice dip or spread for gluten-free toast points or tortilla chips, and a great dip for fresh vegetables.

INGREDIENTS | MAKES 1⅔ CUPS

2 large cloves garlic

1 (19-ounce) can chickpeas

4 tablespoons reserved juice from chickpeas

2 tablespoons, plus 1 teaspoon lemon juice

2 tablespoons tahini or peanut butter

¼ teaspoon ground cumin, or to taste

3 or 4 slices gluten-free bread (such as Udi's Whole Grain) or gluten-free tortilla chips

Replacing Tahini with Peanut Butter

Peanut butter makes a handy (and less expensive!) alternative to tahini in recipes. Both lend a creamy texture and nutty flavor to dishes such as Middle Eastern Hummus. However, tahini, which is made by grinding raw or toasted sesame seeds, is the winner in the nutrition department. While their fat and calorie content are nearly identical, tahini is loaded with vitamins and minerals, such as calcium and lecithin.

1. Preheat oven to 350°F.

2. Smash, peel, and finely chop the garlic cloves. Drain the chickpeas and mash them, reserving the juice from the can.

3. In a small bowl, blend together the chopped garlic, mashed chickpeas, chickpea juice, lemon juice, tahini or peanut butter, and cumin.

4. Place gluten-free bread on a baking sheet and toast in the oven for 8–10 minutes or until crispy. Cut into triangles. Spread a heaping tablespoon of hummus on each triangle. Store the remainder of the hummus in a sealed container in the refrigerator until ready to use.

Classic BLT

Not a fan of tomato? Try substituting finely chopped red bell pepper.
For extra flavor, mix a few pieces of finely chopped red onion with the mayonnaise.

INGREDIENTS | SERVES 1

2 slices bacon

2 lettuce leaves

2 slices gluten-free bread (such as Udi's Whole Grain)

1 tablespoon mayonnaise, or to taste

4 slices tomato

1. Cook the bacon in a frying pan or broiler until crisp. Drain the bacon slices on paper towels and cut into strips about 3" long.

2. Wash the lettuce leaves and drain thoroughly. Break into bite-size pieces. Toast the bread.

3. Spread the mayonnaise on one side of each slice of bread. Lay the bacon strips horizontally on 1 slice of bread on top of the mayonnaise. Lay the tomato slices on top, and then the lettuce. Close the sandwich and cut in half.

Ham and Roasted Red Pepper Sandwich

Not sure which mustard brand to use? Sweet prepared mustards—such as honey mustard—make a nice contrast with the smoky flavor of the roasted red pepper in this recipe.

INGREDIENTS | SERVES 1

2 slices gluten-free bread (such as Udi's Whole Grain)

1 tablespoon light mayonnaise (optional)

Freshly ground black pepper to taste (optional)

2 romaine lettuce leaves

½ roasted red bell pepper (see sidebar)

2 slices cooked ham

1 tablespoon prepared mustard, or to taste

How to Roast a Bell Pepper

Place the pepper on its side (not standing up) on a broiling pan. Brush the top side of the pepper with balsamic vinegar. Turn over and brush the other side with olive oil. Broil the pepper for about 15–20 minutes, turning frequently, until the skin is blackened and charred. Then place the pepper in a sealed plastic bag and leave it for at least 10 minutes. Remove the pepper from the bag and peel off the skin. Remove the stem and the seeds. To serve, cut into cubes or lengthwise into strips.

1. Place the slices of bread on a plate or a paper towel. If using the mayonnaise, spread it over the slices of bread. Sprinkle with pepper, if desired.

2. Wash the lettuce leaves and drain. Cut the roasted red pepper into bite-size pieces.

3. Lay a lettuce leaf on one of the slices of bread. Lay 1 slice of the ham on top of the lettuce and spread some of the mustard on top. Place a few pieces of red pepper on top of the ham, add another piece of lettuce, and add the final piece of ham. Spread the remaining mustard on the final ham slice. Lay the other piece of bread on top of the ingredients and close up the sandwich. Cut the sandwich into 4 quarters.

Vegetarian Red Pepper and Hummus Panini

This delicious vegetarian grilled sandwich is super easy to make and will be a lunch staple in your dorm room. If you don't have a panini maker or a stovetop to use to grill the sandwich, simply toast the bread and make a regular sandwich!

INGREDIENTS | MAKES 1 GLUTEN-FREE PANINI

2 slices gluten-free bread (such as Udi's Whole Grain)

3 tablespoons hummus

¼ cup baby spinach leaves

¼ cup sliced mushrooms, lightly sautéed

3 thin slices avocado

½ red bell pepper, thinly sliced (use about 5 strips)

2–3 tablespoons alfalfa sprouts

Salt and pepper, to taste

Bell Pepper Types

Ever wonder what the difference is between green, orange, and red bell peppers? Actually, all three come from the same plant. The main difference is that red and orange bell peppers have been allowed to ripen longer on the vine. The extra ripening time gives red bell peppers a sweeter flavor than green bell peppers, making them a popular salad ingredient.

1. Lay the 2 slices of bread out on a plate. Spread each slice evenly with the hummus. Layer the remaining ingredients on 1 slice and then top with the other slice.

2. Place the sandwich in a panini maker or George Foreman Grill, or gently toast on a heavy-bottomed cast-iron frying pan and flatten the sandwich by placing a piece of foil on top of the sandwich in the pan and then place another heavy frying pan on top of the foil. Cook on each side for 2–3 minutes over medium-high heat.

3. Serve the panini cut in half with a side of applesauce, carrot sticks, and/or potato chips.

Portobello Mushroom Burger

Earthy-flavored portobello mushrooms are frequently used as a meat substitute by vegetarians.
This recipe makes either a filling lunch or a light dinner.

INGREDIENTS | SERVES 1

1 gluten-free English muffin (such as Food For Life brand), cut in half

4 teaspoons low-fat margarine

1 large portobello mushroom

1 leaf romaine lettuce

1 tablespoon olive oil

3 tablespoons chopped onion, or to taste

1 tomato slice

2 tablespoons grated cheese (such as Swiss or Cheddar)

1. Toast the English muffin halves. Spread 1 teaspoon of the margarine on each half while still warm and set aside. Wipe the portobello mushroom with a damp cloth and cut into thin slices. Wash the lettuce leaf, dry, and tear into pieces.

2. Heat the olive oil on medium in a frying pan. Add the chopped onion and cook on medium-low heat until tender.

3. Add the remaining 2 teaspoons margarine to the frying pan. Push the onion to the side and lay the portobello mushroom slices flat in the pan. Cook until browned on the bottom, about 2 minutes. Turn over and cook the other side until browned. Add the tomato slice to the pan while the mushroom is cooking.

4. When the mushroom slices are browned on both sides, sprinkle the grated cheese on top. Cook briefly until the cheese is melted.

5. To make the burger, lay the tomato on one muffin half and place the cooked onion on the other half. Spread the mushroom and melted cheese mixture on top of both halves. Serve open-faced, garnished with the lettuce.

Roasted Pepper Soup

This healthy soup makes a high-protein lunch. If you're looking for something a bit less filling for a midafternoon snack, simply leave out the chickpeas. You can buy prepared roasted red peppers, which are sometimes called "fire-roasted."

INGREDIENTS | SERVES 1

1 tablespoon olive oil

1 clove garlic, smashed, peeled, and chopped

¼ cup chopped white onion

½ cup sliced mushrooms

2½ cups chicken broth

2 small or medium-size roasted red bell peppers, roughly chopped

¾ cup chickpeas

¼ teaspoon salt

Black or white pepper, to taste

¼ teaspoon dried parsley, or to taste

1. Heat the oil in a medium-size saucepan. Add the garlic and onion. Cook over low-medium heat until the onion is tender. Add the mushrooms and cook for 12 minutes, stirring occasionally.

2. Add the chicken broth and bring to a boil.

3. Add the roasted pepper chunks and the chickpeas. Bring the soup back to a boil.

4. Stir in the salt, pepper, and parsley. Serve hot.

Rainbow Salad with Fennel

Fennel adds a distinct licorice flavor to this standard coleslaw recipe. If you can't find fennel, parsley can stand in as a substitute, but the dish won't have the same flavor.

INGREDIENTS | SERVES 2

1 carrot
1 red bell pepper
2 cups shredded red cabbage
2 tablespoons, plus 2 teaspoons, low-fat mayonnaise
3 teaspoons honey, slightly warmed
1 fennel bulb

1. Wash the carrot and red pepper. Grate the carrot until you have ½–⅔ cup of grated carrot. Cut the red pepper into thin strips.

2. In a large bowl, mix together the carrot, red pepper, and cabbage.

3. In a small bowl, combine the mayonnaise and the honey. Add to the vegetables in the large bowl and toss to combine.

4. Rinse the fennel bulb under running water and pat dry. Cut off the top and bottom of the bulb. Cut into quarters, remove the core, and cut into thin slices. Garnish the coleslaw with the fennel.

Apple and Walnut Salad

This recipe calls for vanilla yogurt, but feel free to experiment with other varieties of vanilla yogurt, such as vanilla with peaches. For added protein, serve with Cheddar cheese slices.

INGREDIENTS | SERVES 1 OR 2

1 celery stalk

1 cup chopped apple (about 1 small apple)

⅓ cup walnut pieces

2 tablespoons vanilla yogurt

Vegetable-Cleaning Tip

Always wash fresh produce just before serving or eating, not when you first store the food in the crisper section of the refrigerator.

1. Wash the celery and cut on the diagonal into 1" pieces.

2. In a medium bowl, combine the celery with the chopped apple and walnut pieces.

3. Toss with the yogurt. Serve immediately, or cover and chill.

Marinated Artichoke Hearts

Serve the marinated artichoke hearts and tomato in a salad or pasta dish, or on top of crusty gluten-free French bread, such as Schar's gluten-free baguettes. If you prefer to leave out the tomato, reduce the olive oil to ¼ cup.

INGREDIENTS | SERVES 1 OR 2

4 canned artichoke hearts

½ tomato

⅓ cup extra-virgin olive oil

1 tablespoon lemon juice

⅛ teaspoon garlic powder

Salt and freshly ground black pepper, to taste

1. Squeeze any excess juice from the canned artichokes. Wash the tomato, pat dry, and slice.

2. In a small bowl, combine the olive oil, lemon juice, garlic powder, and salt and pepper to create a marinade.

3. Pour the marinade into a resealable plastic bag. Add the artichokes and tomatoes and seal the bag. Refrigerate overnight to give the flavors a chance to blend.

Easy Steamed Turkey Breast for One

Delicious, healthy, and so easy to prepare, this turkey is great served with mashed potatoes and vegetables or even shredded and made into turkey salad.

INGREDIENTS | SERVES 1

2 (3-ounce) boneless turkey breast fillets
1 cup gluten-free chicken broth
1 cup water
1 teaspoon dried rosemary
½ cup baby carrots

1. Preheat the over to 350°F.

2. Rinse the turkey fillets under running water and pat dry.

3. Layer all the ingredients in a casserole dish. Cover with aluminum foil and bake for 35 minutes or until the turkey is cooked through (when the juices run clear from the turkey).

Spring Roll Salad

Many of the ingredients that are traditionally found in spring rolls make a flavorful salad.

INGREDIENTS | SERVES 2–4

1 cup mung bean sprouts
1 carrot
1 red bell pepper
1 (14-ounce) can baby corn
2 teaspoons olive oil
3 teaspoons gluten-free soy sauce (such as La Choy)
1 tablespoon red wine vinegar
1 teaspoon sugar

1. Wash the vegetables. Drain the mung bean sprouts thoroughly. Peel the carrot and cut into thin strips about 2" long. Cut the red pepper in half, remove the seeds, and cut into thin strips about 2" long. Rinse the baby corn in warm water and drain thoroughly.

2. Combine the olive oil, soy sauce, red wine vinegar, and sugar in a jar and shake well.

3. Toss the salad with the dressing. Wait about 30 minutes before serving to give the flavors a chance to blend.

Mom's Egg Salad Sandwich

You may be in college, but that doesn't mean you can't make yourself a mean egg salad sandwich—just like Mom's.

INGREDIENTS | SERVES 4

6 hard-boiled eggs

½ cup fat-free Miracle Whip salad dressing or your favorite mayonnaise (such as Duke's or Hellman's)

¼ cup finely chopped celery

2 tablespoons finely chopped flat-leaf parsley

Salt and pepper, to taste

1. Separate the hard-boiled egg whites from the yolks. Finely chop the egg whites.

2. Press the egg yolks through a sieve and add to chopped egg whites in small bowl.

3. Add the salad dressing, celery, and parsley and blend well. Season with salt and pepper to taste.

4. Chill mixture for 1 hour. Spread on your favorite gluten-free bread.

Tropical Cobb Salad

The mango, feta, and pine nuts in this salad offer incredible textural differences yet perfectly complementary flavors.

INGREDIENTS | SERVES 1

2 cups chopped romaine lettuce

3 ounces cooked chicken breast

¼ cup plum tomatoes

2 tablespoons chopped mango

½ tablespoon toasted pine nuts

1 tablespoon feta cheese

Combine all the ingredients in a large bowl. Choose a low-fat citrus dressing to serve on the side.

Fantastic Feta

Feta is a brined curd cheese traditionally made in Greece. It is an aged cheese, commonly produced in blocks, and has a slightly grainy texture. It is often used in salads (ever heard of Greek salad?), some types of pastries, and other baked dishes.

Greek Salad

The Greek diet is associated with a decreased risk of cancer. To pursue Mediterranean-style eating habits, enjoy olives, fruit, beans, and fish on a regular basis.

INGREDIENTS | SERVES 1

2 cups chopped romaine lettuce

¼ cup diced tomatoes

2 tablespoons diced cucumbers

2 kalamata olives

2 pepperoncini

2 tablespoons diced red onion

¼ cup bell pepper slices

1 tablespoon feta cheese

Combine all ingredients in a bowl. Serve with Greek dressing on the side.

Healthy Taco Salad

Use caution when ordering this at a restaurant. Taco salads are often comprised of fatty ground beef, full-fat cheese, sour cream, and a fried, full-gluten tortilla shell. For a vegetarian version of this recipe, use 1 cup of peeled, cooked, and diced sweet potatoes instead of ground turkey.

INGREDIENTS | SERVES 1

2 cups chopped romaine lettuce

3 ounces lean ground turkey, cooked

2 tablespoons diced tomatoes

2 tablespoons black beans

2 tablespoons onions, caramelized

2 tablespoons corn

1 tablespoon shredded low-fat Cheddar cheese

1 jalapeño pepper, sliced

Layer all the ingredients in a bowl. Serve with salsa.

German-Style Potato Salad

This recipe is exceptionally tasty and is wonderful when served with barbecued meats.

INGREDIENTS | SERVES 4

2 large Idaho, Russet, or Yukon Gold potatoes

¼ cup cider vinegar

¼ cup vegetable oil

1 teaspoon salt

1 teaspoon pepper

1 teaspoon sugar

1 teaspoon Hungarian sweet paprika

1 red onion, chopped

2 scallions, chopped

½ cup chopped fresh parsley

1. Peel the potatoes and cut into ½" slices.

2. Boil the potatoes in enough salted water to cover for 10–15 minutes or until just softened.

3. Mix the rest of the ingredients in a large bowl. Drain potatoes and add to the dressing immediately. Toss gently to coat. Serve hot or cold.

Picnic Time

As with any cold potato or gluten-free macaroni salad, this dish is a great option to bring to your next picnic or barbecue. And unlike salads that include dairy or mayonnaise, this one will last a little longer out on the picnic table.

Creamy Corn Chowder

This hearty soup makes a cozy meal on a cold day.

INGREDIENTS | SERVES 6

1 tablespoon oil

1 small onion, finely chopped

3 medium potatoes, peeled and chopped

2 cups water

½ teaspoon salt

¼ teaspoon black pepper

2 tablespoons cornstarch

2 (15-ounce) cans corn, drained

2 cups milk

2 tablespoons butter or margarine

Is It Done Yet?

To test potatoes for doneness, insert a fork into a few different cooked potatoes. If the fork goes in easily, they are done.

1. In a large saucepan, heat the oil over medium heat. Add the onion and cook for about 5 minutes, stirring frequently.

2. Add the potatoes, water, salt, and pepper. Turn up the heat until the mixture begins to boil. Reduce it to a simmer and continue to cook for about 20 minutes or until the potatoes are tender.

3. In a separate bowl, mix the cornstarch with a little cold water to avoid clumps.

4. Add the corn, milk, and butter or margarine to the soup. Stir in the cornstarch-water mixture to help thicken the soup. Continue simmering for another 20 minutes, stirring occasionally.

5. Cool slightly before serving. Try your chowder with a salad and fruit for a complete meal.

Tasty Tomato Soup

*This is the perfect side to a gluten-free grilled cheese sandwich,
and also great to pack for a hot lunch at school.*

INGREDIENTS | SERVES 4

10–12 ripe tomatoes
1 tablespoon oil
½ cup chopped onion
3 cloves garlic, minced
1¾ cups gluten-free vegetable broth
1 (6-ounce) can tomato paste
1 teaspoon dried basil

How to Peel Tomatoes

With a sharp knife, cut an "X" into the bottom of each tomato. Place tomatoes in boiling water for 30–60 seconds. Using a slotted spoon, remove them from the boiling water and place in a bowl of ice water. Once they have cooled for a few minutes, the skins will peel right off.

1. Peel and chop the tomatoes, then place them in a large bowl and set them aside.

2. In a large saucepan, heat the oil over medium heat. Add the onion and garlic and cook for about 3 minutes or until the onion is tender.

3. Add the tomatoes, cover the pan, and cook for about 5 minutes to soften the tomatoes.

4. Add the vegetable broth and tomato paste. Bring the mixture to a boil over high heat, and then reduce it to a simmer. Cover the pan and cook for another 10–15 minutes.

5. Pour the soup into a blender or food processor, 1 cup at a time. Do not overfill the blender. (If you put too much into the blender at once, the hot liquid will overflow when you turn it on.) Blend the mixture until it is smooth.

6. Pour blended soup into serving bowls to serve and sprinkle with basil. Continue with remaining portions. It may be helpful to prepare this soup in advance and transfer the blended soup to a new saucepan on the stove to keep warm.

Grilled Cheese and Tomato Sandwich

What's better than a warm and crispy grilled cheese sandwich?
Here's a slightly different spin on the old favorite that makes it more nutritious, too.

INGREDIENTS | SERVES 1

2 teaspoons butter

2 slices gluten-free bread (such as Udi's Whole Grain)

1 slice Cheddar cheese

1 or 2 thin slices tomato

1. Spread the butter on one side of each slice of bread. Make a sandwich with the cheese and tomato between the 2 slices of bread, with the butter on the outside of the sandwich.

2. Place the sandwich in a frying pan over medium heat and cook it for about 2 minutes on each side or until the cheese is melted and the bread becomes slightly browned and crispy.

Mini Pizza in a Flash

A mini pizza is about the quickest lunch you can make. It doesn't require many ingredients,
and it's easy to personalize it to your liking. Most of the products that are called for in this recipe are
naturally gluten-free, but you will want to read the ingredients label before using to double check.

INGREDIENTS | MAKES 2 MINI PIZZAS

1 gluten-free bagel, split in half

2 tablespoons pizza, spaghetti, or tomato sauce

¼ cup shredded mozzarella cheese

Meat or vegetable toppings (optional)

1. Preheat the oven to 350°F.

2. Place the bagel halves on a cookie sheet. Spread the pizza sauce over each bagel half. Top with mozzarella cheese and other toppings.

3. Bake for 5–8 minutes or until the cheese is melted.

Cheesiest Macaroni and Cheese

Giving up gluten also means giving up the macaroni and cheese from a box.
This homemade version makes a comforting, warm meal or a great cold lunch.

INGREDIENTS | SERVES 4

1 cup uncooked gluten-free elbow macaroni

2 tablespoons butter or margarine

1 tablespoon cornstarch

¼ teaspoon salt

¼ teaspoon pepper

¼ teaspoon dry mustard

¼ teaspoon gluten-free Worcestershire sauce

1 cup milk

1½ cups shredded sharp Cheddar cheese

2 tablespoons crushed gluten-free corn flakes

1. Preheat the oven to 275°F.

2. Cook macaroni in a large pot of water according to package directions. Drain in a colander.

3. Melt the butter or margarine in a large saucepan over medium heat. Reduce the heat to low. Add the cornstarch, salt, pepper, mustard, and Worcestershire sauce. Stir until smooth.

4. Add the milk and cheese. Continue stirring until the cheese melts and the sauce is creamy and smooth.

5. Stir the macaroni into the cheese sauce.

6. Pour the mixture into a 2-quart casserole dish. Top with the crushed corn flakes.

7. Bake for 30–40 minutes or until the casserole is heated through and lightly browned. Let the casserole dish sit for about 5–10 minutes before serving so the cheesy, creamy sauce has a chance to thicken.

Colorful Grilled Corn Salad

*Although this salad is great paired with beef, chicken, or fish,
it is also terrific with just gluten-free tortilla chips.*

INGREDIENTS | SERVES 8

6 ears corn, shucked and cleaned

1 (19-ounce) can black beans, drained and rinsed

1 red bell pepper, chopped

½ cup diced red onion

½ cup chopped fresh cilantro

1 jalapeño pepper, finely diced (optional)

½ cup olive oil

½ cup red wine vinegar

2 tablespoons lime juice

1 tablespoon agave nectar or sugar

1 teaspoon salt

1 clove garlic, minced

½ teaspoon ground cumin

½ teaspoon ground black pepper

1 teaspoon chili powder

Dash of hot sauce

1. Grill corn over medium heat for 15–20 minutes, turning occasionally, or until slightly blackened in areas. Allow to cool and then cut off corn kernels into a bowl. Add black beans, red pepper, red onion, cilantro, and jalapeño pepper.

2. In a small bowl, whisk together the olive oil, red wine vinegar, lime juice, agave nectar or sugar, salt, garlic, cumin, black pepper, chili powder, and hot sauce.

3. Pour over corn mixture and stir to coat.

4. Refrigerate for at least 1 hour before serving.

Great for Parties and Potlucks

This salad is the perfect dish to bring to the next barbecue or potluck that you attend. The dish is not only gluten-free but also free from dairy, peanuts, tree nuts, fish and shellfish, eggs, and soy.

Waldorf-Inspired Quinoa Salad

This salad is tasty but also very healthy. It can be served as a side dish, dessert, or even breakfast!

INGREDIENTS | SERVES 6

1 cup water
1 cup apple juice
½ teaspoon ground cinnamon
1 cup quinoa, well rinsed and drained
1 large red apple, cored and diced
1 cup chopped celery
½ cup dried cranberries
½ cup chopped walnuts
1 cup vanilla yogurt

1. Place water, apple juice, cinnamon, and quinoa in medium saucepan and bring to a boil. Reduce heat and simmer for 15–20 minutes or until the liquid is absorbed. Cool, cover, and refrigerate quinoa for at least 1 hour.

2. Add apple, celery, cranberries, and walnuts to cooled quinoa. Mix well. Fold in the yogurt. Refrigerate until ready to serve.

Garden Medley Salad

This salad can be served as is, or you can toss it with mixed greens or fresh spinach.
Cooked chicken or ham can be added to make this a main-dish salad.

INGREDIENTS | SERVES 4

1 cup sliced carrots

3 stalks celery, chopped

1 cup small cauliflower florets

¼ cup chopped green onion

1 yellow bell pepper, chopped

1 cup cherry tomatoes

1 cup chopped cucumber

⅓ cup gluten-free Italian salad dressing

In a medium bowl, combine all ingredients except salad dressing and toss to blend. Drizzle salad dressing over all and toss to coat. Serve immediately, or cover and chill 2–3 hours before serving to blend flavors.

Vegetables for Salads

Most vegetables can be used raw in salads, as long as they are sliced thinly, broken, or cut into small pieces. If you'd like, you could blanch the vegetables before adding to the salad. To blanch, drop the prepared vegetables into boiling water for 30–40 seconds, and then immediately plunge into ice water to stop the cooking.

Antioxidant Fruit and Nut Salad

Stress from school starting to make you feel run down? This salad is your ticket—the berries are packed full of antioxidants, and walnuts have one of the best omega profiles for nuts to reduce inflammation.

INGREDIENTS | SERVES 2

½ cup sliced strawberries
½ cup raspberries
½ cup blackberries
½ cup blueberries
½ cup dried mulberries
½ cup chopped walnuts

Combine all ingredients and enjoy.

Stuffed Tomatoes

This is a great vegetarian lunch option that is packed with flavor.

INGREDIENTS | SERVES 3

3 large beefsteak tomatoes
6 small button mushrooms, sliced
4 cloves garlic, minced
6 sun-dried tomatoes, chopped
1 teaspoon ground black pepper
½ teaspoon paprika
1 teaspoon thyme
8 leaves fresh basil, torn

1. Preheat oven to 350°F.

2. Hollow out the tomatoes, reserving tomato pulp. Place tomatoes in a small baking dish.

3. Mix tomato pulp with mushrooms, garlic, sun-dried tomatoes, pepper, paprika, thyme, and basil.

4. Fill tomatoes with tomato-pulp mixture and bake for 25 minutes.

Tuna Salad with a Kick

Tuna is a great lunch or snack. It is naturally low in fat, low in calories, and delicious!

INGREDIENTS | SERVES 3

2 (7-ounce) cans chunk light tuna in water
20 green olives, chopped
½ cup chopped green onions
3 tablespoons capers
1 jalapeño pepper, finely chopped
1 red bell pepper, chopped
2 tablespoons olive oil
2 tablespoons red chili flakes
Juice of 3 lemons

1. Mix all ingredients in a large bowl.

2. Serve chilled, alone or over lettuce greens.

Curried Chicken Salad

This recipe makes two servings, but you can double or triple the amounts for a larger group. You can also substitute different spices for more variety.

INGREDIENTS | SERVES 2

2 tablespoons olive oil
8 ounces chicken breast, cubed
1 stalk celery, sliced
1 small onion, diced
½ English cucumber, diced
½ cup chopped almonds
2 apples, chopped
½ teaspoon curry powder
4 cups baby romaine lettuce

1. In a frying pan, heat olive oil and cook the chicken, celery, and onion for 5–10 minutes or until chicken is thoroughly cooked. Set aside to cool.

2. In a mixing bowl, combine the cucumber, almonds, apples, and curry powder with the cooled chicken mixture.

3. Serve over bed of baby romaine lettuce.

Zesty Pecan Chicken and Grape Salad

Coating your chicken with nuts adds a crispy skin to keep the breast inside moist and tender.

INGREDIENTS | SERVES 6

¼ cup chopped pecans

1 teaspoon chili powder

¼ cup olive oil

1½ pounds boneless, skinless chicken breasts

1½ cups white grapes

6 cups salad greens

Toasting Nuts for Fresher Flavor and Crispness

To wake the natural flavor of the nuts, heat them on the stovetop or in the oven for a few minutes. For the stovetop, spread nuts in a dry frying pan, and heat over medium heat until their natural oils come to the surface. For the oven, spread the nuts in a single layer on a baking sheet and toast at 350°F for 5–10 minutes or until the oils are visible. Cool nuts before serving.

1. Preheat the oven to 400°F.

2. In a blender, mix the pecans and chili powder. Pour in the oil while the blender is running. When the mixture is thoroughly combined, pour it into a shallow bowl.

3. Coat the chicken with the pecan mixture and place on racked baking dish. Roast for 40–50 minutes or until the chicken is thoroughly cooked. Remove from oven, let cool for 5 minutes, and thinly slice.

4. Slice the grapes and tear the greens into bite-size pieces. To serve, fan the chicken over the greens and sprinkle with sliced grapes.

Avocado Chicken Salad

This recipe makes a great party salad. You can serve it in lettuce cups for a meal or in small cups with spoons as an appetizer.

INGREDIENTS | SERVES 3

3 avocados, pitted and peeled

2 boneless, skinless chicken breasts, cooked and shredded

½ red onion, chopped

1 large tomato, chopped

¼ cup chopped cilantro

Juice of 1 large lime

1. In a medium bowl, mash the avocados. Add the chicken and mix well.

2. Add the onion, tomato, cilantro, and lime juice to the avocado-and-chicken mixture. Mix well and serve.

CHAPTER 4

Party Grub

Artichoke and Spinach Dip

For a perfect party snack, serve this dip with gluten-free breads and crackers.
You can make this in advance and then warm it up at the last minute.

INGREDIENTS | MAKES 2 CUPS

1 (10-ounce) package frozen chopped spinach, thawed

2 tablespoons olive oil

1 (12-ounce) jar artichoke hearts, drained and chopped

4 ounces cream cheese

8 ounces sour cream

1 teaspoon garlic powder

½ bunch scallions, chopped

2 tablespoons fresh lemon juice

¼ teaspoon freshly grated nutmeg

1. Drain the thawed spinach, squeezing it with paper towels until extra liquid is gone.

2. Heat the olive oil and add the spinach. Cook until it is just soft, about 5 minutes.

3. Remove the pan from the heat and add the rest of the ingredients, stirring to mix. Serve warm or cold.

How to Cook Fresh Artichokes

To cook fresh artichokes, simply snip off the edges of the leaves and cut off about ½" from the top. Place the trimmed artichokes in a large saucepan and cover them with water. Add a few slices of lemon and a clove of garlic to the cooking water. Cover and cook over medium-high heat for 25–35 minutes or until the artichoke leaves are tender. Drain off water and eat the outer leaves by dipping them in butter or your favorite dressing and scraping them with your teeth. When you get to the fuzzy "choke," simply remove the fuzzy part and then eat the artichoke heart by cutting into small pieces.

Spicy Gorgonzola Dip with Red Pepper "Spoons"

This is very flavorful—the more fresh herbs, the better. Try using fresh chives, basil, and oregano.

INGREDIENTS | MAKES 2 CUPS

6 ounces Gorgonzola cheese, at room temperature

4 ounces mayonnaise

4 ounces cream cheese, at room temperature

2 ounces jarred roasted red peppers

2 teaspoons chopped fresh herbs (such as oregano, basil, and chives)

Salt, black pepper, and Tabasco sauce, to taste

4 red bell peppers

1. Put all the ingredients except the 4 red bell peppers into the food processor and blend until smooth. Scrape into a serving bowl.

2. Wash, core, and seed the peppers, and then cut into chunks (these will be your "spoons"). Place the red pepper spoons around the dip.

Exciting and Distinctive—and Healthy—Party Fare

Many of the party appetizers in this chapter are less fattening than plain old cheese and crackers. They are definitely not ho-hum, and many are full of healthful vitamins, minerals, and phytochemicals. Bright red and yellow peppers are an excellent source of vitamin C.

Sweet Potato Chips

Sweet potatoes are loaded with vitamin A and very delicious when fried and salted.

INGREDIENTS | MAKES ABOUT 3 DOZEN CHIPS

2 large sweet potatoes, peeled
3 cups canola oil
Salt and pepper, to taste

1. Slice the potatoes thinly.

2. Heat the oil in a large frying pan to 375°F.

3. Fry the potato slices for about 3–4 minutes, depending on the thickness of the slices. When the chips are very crisp, remove from the oil and drain.

4. Add salt and pepper. Serve with a dip or eat plain.

Mini Quiches

Mini quiches make a wonderful party snack. You can vary the ingredients, using Cheddar cheese instead of Jarlsberg and chopped, cooked bacon instead of ham.

INGREDIENTS | MAKES 12 MINI QUICHES

1 package gluten-free piecrust mix (such as Gluten Free Pantry)
2 eggs
½ cup grated Jarlsberg cheese
¼ cup minced prosciutto or smoked ham
⅔ cup cream
⅛ teaspoon grated nutmeg
2 tablespoons minced fresh chives
Freshly ground black pepper, to taste

1. Preheat the oven to 325°F. Spray a mini-muffin pan with nonstick spray.

2. Prepare the piecrust mix according to box directions. Roll out thinly. Dip the rim of a juice glass or a 2" biscuit cutter in rice flour, cut dough into 12 rounds, and line the muffin cups with dough.

3. Mix the rest of the ingredients in a food processor.

4. Fill the cups three-quarters full with the cheese mixture.

5. Bake for about 10 minutes or until the quiches are set. Let rest for 5 minutes. Carefully lift the mini quiches from the cups. Serve warm.

Golden Parmesan Crisps

It's important to use a block of fresh Parmesan cheese in this recipe; the bottled stuff won't work as well because it's too fine and too dry. Use the coarse grating blade of a food processor or a box grater.

INGREDIENTS | MAKES 12 CRISPS

2 tablespoons unsalted butter (more if necessary)

12 heaping tablespoons coarsely grated fresh Parmesan cheese

Freshly ground black or cayenne pepper, to taste

1. Heat the butter in a pan over medium heat until it bubbles.

2. Spoon the cheese by tablespoonfuls over the butter, pressing down lightly with the back of the spoon to spread.

3. After about 2 minutes, turn and sauté until both sides are lightly golden brown. Add more butter if necessary.

4. Sprinkle with black pepper, cayenne, or both. Serve immediately.

Baby Back Ribs

You can use Asian or any kind of gluten-free barbecue sauce you wish. The trick is to cook the ribs in the sauce. Make sure to read the product labels carefully, as some barbecue sauces are thickened with wheat flour.

INGREDIENTS | SERVES 4–6

4 pounds baby back ribs, cut into 1-rib servings

2 tablespoons vegetable oil

1 cup gluten-free barbecue sauce (such as Sticky Fingers, KC Masterpiece, or Sweet Baby Ray's)

1 cup tomato juice

½ cup orange juice

1. In a large frying pan, brown the ribs in the vegetable oil over medium-high heat until lightly brown, making sure to turn them as they cook.

2. Add the rest of the ingredients and cover. Cook over very low heat for 1 hour.

3. Remove the ribs and continue cooking the sauce until reduced to 1 cup. Serve ribs with sauce for dipping.

Chili Bean Dip with Dipping Vegetables

This is a great addition to any snack tray, whether for watching a game on TV or after class.

INGREDIENTS | MAKES 1 QUART

½ pound ground beef

1 onion, chopped

2 jalapeño peppers (or to taste), cored, seeded, and chopped

2 cloves garlic, chopped

2 tablespoons vegetable oil

4 teaspoons chili powder, or to taste

1 (13-ounce) can crushed tomatoes with juice

1 (13-ounce) can red kidney beans

½ cup gluten-free beer (such as Redbridge, Bard's Tale, or New Grist) (You can leave this out if gluten-free beer is not available in your area)

Assortment of carrots, celery pieces, radishes, broccoli, spears of zucchini, etc.

1. In a large frying pan over medium heat, sauté the beef and vegetables in the oil, breaking up with a spoon to avoid clumping.

2. When the vegetables are soft, add the rest of the ingredients (except the vegetables for dipping). Cover and simmer for 1 hour.

3. Serve warm, or let it cool and turn this into a dip by pulsing it in the food processor. Do not make it smooth. Serve alongside veggies.

Chili and Beans

There are endless variations of the chili-and-bean combination. Some people use turkey; others add dark chocolate and cinnamon and vary the amounts of beans and tomatoes. Some forms of chili don't have any beans. Different regions use various amounts of spice, heat, and ingredients.

Grilled Curried Chicken Wings

Traditional Buffalo wings are generally fried. These are a lot less fattening, done with a rub and some olive oil. Double the recipe and refrigerate half for delicious cold snacks.

INGREDIENTS | SERVES 4–8

4 pounds chicken wings, split at the joint, tips removed

1 tablespoon curry powder, or to taste

1 tablespoon onion powder

1 tablespoon garlic powder

¼ teaspoon cinnamon

2 teaspoons dark brown sugar

¼ cup freshly squeezed lime juice

¼ cup olive oil

1 teaspoon salt

Ground black pepper, to taste

1. Rinse the wings and set them on paper towels to dry.

2. In a large bowl, mix the rest of the ingredients together. Coat the chicken with the curry mixture, cover, and refrigerate for 1 hour.

3. Grill chicken over medium-hot coals or broil at 350°F for 20 minutes, turning every few minutes, or until well browned.

Make-Ahead Chicken Wings

Want to make a batch of chicken wings ahead of time to serve to a crowd? Cook the chicken wings according to the recipe, place in freezer bags, and seal. Mark the date the wings were frozen. When ready to use, thaw the frozen chicken wings in the refrigerator. Cooked chicken wings (and leftover unused sauce) can be frozen for up to 1 month.

Fried Polenta Squares with Salsa

Make the polenta a day in advance, and then refrigerate it until just before the party.

INGREDIENTS | MAKES 12–24 SQUARES

6½ cups water

2 tablespoons salt

2 cups yellow gluten-free cornmeal (such as Bob's Red Mill)

2–4 ounces unsalted butter

2 tablespoons dried herbs or 1 tablespoon each fresh basil, rosemary, and parsley

½ cup freshly grated Parmesan cheese

Freshly ground black pepper, to taste

2 tablespoons unsalted butter and 2–4 tablespoons vegetable oil, for frying

1 (8-ounce) jar of your favorite salsa or homemade guacamole for dipping

1. Bring the water to a boil.

2. Add salt, and using your hand, drop the cornmeal into the boiling water, letting it slip slowly between your fingers to make a very slim stream. You should be able to see each grain. Do not dump the cornmeal into the water or you will get a glue-like mass.

3. Stir constantly while adding the cornmeal. Reduce heat to a simmer and keep stirring for about 20 minutes as it thickens.

4. Stir in the 2–4 ounces butter, herbs, Parmesan cheese, and pepper. Spread in a 9" × 13" glass pan that has been prepared with nonstick spray.

5. Chill for 3 hours or overnight.

6. Cut into squares. Fry the squares over medium heat in a combination of butter and oil and fry until golden brown. If you are having an outdoor party, you can grill the squares over low flame for a smoky flavor. Serve with salsa or guacamole.

Cheese Fondue with Dipping Vegetables

This is an "interactive" party appetizer, or you can serve it as a main course.

INGREDIENTS | SERVES 12–14

1 clove garlic

1 cup dry white wine

1 pound imported Swiss cheese (such as Jarlsberg), coarsely grated

¼ teaspoon ground nutmeg

Freshly ground pepper, to taste

3 tablespoons maraschino cherry juice

Salt, to taste

2 egg yolks, beaten

2 tablespoons gluten-free flour (such as brown rice flour or arrowroot starch)

½ cup cream

2 tablespoons butter

1 loaf gluten-free French-style bread, cubed and toasted

1 broccoli crown, blanched in boiling water for 2 minutes, cooled and cut in pieces

2 red bell peppers, cored, seeded, and cut into chunks

½ pound sugar snap peas, rinsed

2 zucchini and/or 12 very thin asparagus tips, cut into pieces

1. Mash the garlic. In a large earthenware pot or chafing dish over a burner, heat the garlic in the wine.

2. Stir in the cheese, nutmeg, pepper, cherry juice, and salt. Mix slowly over low flame.

3. In a separate bowl, whisk together the egg yolks, gluten-free flour, and cream. Stir into the cheese mixture.

4. Serve with buttered bread cubes and vegetables, keeping the heat low under the chafing dish water basin. Or, if you are using a heavy flameproof earthenware casserole, keep a low flame under it.

5. When the cheese mixture has melted, enjoy by spearing veggies or bread onto a long-handled fork and dipping into the cheese mixture. If the cheese gets too thick, add a bit more warm white wine.

Fondue Facts

Ever wonder where fondue came from? It was first created in Switzerland as a way of using up hardened cheese. Traditionally a peasant dish, fondue became popular in America in the 1950s as a result of Chef Konrad Egli serving it at his restaurant Chalet Swiss. Later on came chocolate fondue.

Puffy Dumplings

These dumplings can be used in any soup you like—not only in Asian recipes but also in Mediterranean vegetable soups and even in Hungarian goulash.

INGREDIENTS | SERVES 4

¼ cup brown rice flour
1 teaspoon baking powder
½ teaspoon black pepper, or to taste
1 teaspoon dried chopped chives
4–5 teaspoons milk
1 egg, beaten

1. In a medium bowl, mix the rice flour, baking powder, black pepper, and chopped chives.

2. Stir in the milk and egg until a stiff dough is formed.

3. Drop by half-teaspoonfuls into hot soup. Stir gently so that the dumplings cook evenly.

Crispy Potato Pancakes

These are amazing with applesauce or sour cream, or alongside eggs. If you prefer to bake the pancakes (to use less oil and have fewer calories), simply place the formed pancakes on a baking sheet lined with parchment paper, brush each cake lightly with a little olive oil, and bake for 25 minutes at 350°F.

INGREDIENTS | MAKES ABOUT 10 PANCAKES

4 Idaho potatoes, peeled and coarsely grated
2 onions, finely chopped
2 eggs, well beaten
½ cup arrowroot starch or tapioca starch
Salt and pepper, to taste
2 cups cooking oil (such as canola)
Sour cream, applesauce, fruit preserves, salsa, or chutney, for garnish

1. In a large bowl, mix the grated potatoes, onions, and eggs. Sprinkle with arrowroot starch or tapioca starch and salt and pepper.

2. In a large frying pan, heat the oil to 350°F. Add the potato mixture by spoonfuls, pressing down each to make a patty.

3. Fry until golden, about 5 minutes per side. Drain, keep warm, and serve with garnish of choice.

Fried Potato Balls

You can hide surprises inside these treats, such as olives, halved cherry tomatoes, or cubes of cheese.

INGREDIENTS | MAKES 8–12 BALLS

3 eggs, separated, whites whisked stiff

1¾ cups finely grated Parmesan cheese, divided

¼ cup arrowroot starch or tapioca starch (more if the mixture is loose or wet)

Salt and pepper, to taste

1½ cups boiled, riced potatoes

2 cups oil, for frying

1. In a large bowl, beat together the egg yolks, 1 cup of the Parmesan cheese, arrowroot starch or tapioca starch, salt and pepper, and potatoes.

2. Fold in the whisked egg whites.

3. Form the mixture into balls about the size of large marbles. Roll in remaining Parmesan cheese. If balls are too soft, place on a cookie sheet in the freezer for a few minutes.

4. Bring oil to 375°F. Carefully add the balls and fry until well browned.

5. Drain on paper towels, and serve hot.

Italian Sausages on Quartered Bell Peppers

*A little sausage goes a long way. Choose between sweet and spicy sausage
in this recipe, or mix the two, depending on your taste.*

INGREDIENTS | MAKES 16 SAUSAGE ROUNDS

1 pound Italian sausages, hot or sweet

4 large red or green bell peppers, cored, seeded, and cut into quarters

Secrets of Italian Sausage

A top-notch Italian sausage will have little fat, so little, in fact, that you may have to add oil to the frying pan when you cook it. When making meatballs, mix ½ pound of the sausage with the meat for the meat-balls and you will be surprised at the difference.

1. Place whole sausages in a pot with enough water to cover, then bring to a rolling boil. Reduce the heat and simmer for 10 minutes.

2. Remove sausages from water. Grill on high heat until nicely browned all over. Cut in rounds and serve on "spoons" of red or green pepper.

Stuffed Olive Appetizer

*This simple appetizer takes mere minutes to make and doesn't require any cooking.
The exact amount of olives used will depend on their size—the recipe can easily be halved if desired.*

INGREDIENTS | MAKES 48 OLIVES

2 teaspoons white wine vinegar

¼ teaspoon garlic powder

¼ cup ricotta cheese

48 extra-large black pitted olives

Stuffing Olives

Stuffing with soft cheese is a great way to add flavor to large olives that have had their pits removed. Besides ricotta cheese, olives can be filled with cream cheese, blue, or even crumbled feta cheese. To fill the olive, all you need is a butter knife; however, a piping bag can also be used. For a fancier appearance, cut a thin slice off the bottom of each olive before filling, so that it can stand upright.

1. In a medium bowl, stir the white wine vinegar and garlic powder into the ricotta cheese.

2. Drain the olives and wipe dry. Use a butter knife to gently force a small amount of the cheese mixture into the olive (depending on the size, each olive will take between ⅛ and ¼ teaspoon). Serve immediately.

Stuffed Mushroom Appetizer

A nice way to finish off these mushrooms after baking is to broil them briefly until the cream cheese is golden brown.

INGREDIENTS | SERVES 12

24 white button mushrooms
1 tablespoon prepared horseradish
4 ounces cream cheese, divided
2 teaspoons lemon juice
⅛ teaspoon chili powder

1. Preheat the oven to 350°F.

2. Wipe the mushrooms clean with a damp cloth. Remove the stems, carefully working the edge of each stem with a knife so that you can pull it right out.

3. In a small bowl, mix the prepared horseradish with half of the cream cheese. In another small bowl, mix the lemon juice and chili powder with the remaining cream cheese.

4. Spoon approximately 1 level teaspoon of cream cheese and horseradish filling into 12 of the mushroom caps (the exact amount of filling needed will depend on the size of the mushroom). Spoon the same amount of the cream cheese and lemon juice filling into the other 12 mushroom caps. Place the mushrooms on an ungreased baking sheet.

5. Bake for 10–12 minutes or until the cream cheese is heated through.

Stuffed Potatoes with Spinach

These can be prepared a few hours in advance.
Cover tightly with plastic wrap and store in the refrigerator until ready to cook.

INGREDIENTS | SERVES 8

8 large baking potatoes (about 8 ounces each)

4 cups fresh spinach leaves

2 teaspoons vegetable oil

1 cup sour cream

½ cup (1 stick) butter or margarine

2 teaspoons garlic powder

2 teaspoons salt

Pepper, to taste

½ cup shredded Monterey jack cheese

1. Preheat oven to 400°F.

2. Wash the potatoes, scrubbing off any dirt. Pierce the potatoes in several spots with a fork. Wash the spinach leaves, drain, and chop.

3. Bake the potatoes for 45 minutes or until done. To test for doneness, pierce the potatoes with a fork. It should go through easily. Remove from the oven.

4. While the potatoes are cooking, heat the oil in a frying pan. Briefly sauté the spinach leaves until bright green.

5. Slice the potatoes lengthwise. Carefully scoop out most of the potato pulp, leaving about ¼" around the skin. Place the potato pulp in a large bowl and mash. Mash in the spinach, sour cream, butter, garlic powder, salt, and pepper.

6. Place the potato shells on a baking sheet. Spoon an even amount of the potato mixture into each shell. Sprinkle each potato with 1 tablespoon shredded cheese. Place in the oven and bake for another 15 minutes or until the cheese is melted.

Buffalo Wings

Buffalo wings are always a hit at parties! Just be sure to keep lots of napkins nearby.

INGREDIENTS | SERVES 5 OR 6

2 pounds chicken wings (about 10–12 wings)

¼ teaspoon black pepper

About 4 cups oil, for deep-frying

5 tablespoons butter or margarine

2 teaspoons white vinegar

¼ cup hot sauce (such as Tabasco)

1 cup blue cheese dressing (If you cannot find gluten-free blue cheese dressing, use ranch instead.)

No-Fry Buffalo Wings

Not comfortable with deep-frying? These buffalo wings can also be baked. Preheat the oven to 350°F and bake for 1 hour or until the wings are cooked. To make sure you have lots of sauce to brush on the baking wings, increase the amounts to 7 tablespoons butter or margarine, 3 teaspoons vinegar, and 6 tablespoons hot sauce.

1. Rinse the chicken wings under cold, running water and pat dry with paper towels. Sprinkle with the black pepper.

2. Set up your wok or deep-fryer according to the manufacturer's instructions, and heat the oil to 360°F.

3. While waiting for the oil to heat, bring the butter or margarine, vinegar, and hot sauce to a boil in a small saucepan. Keep warm on low heat until needed.

4. Deep-fry the chicken wings until browned and cooked through. Remove the wings and drain on paper towels.

5. Brush with the hot sauce. Serve with the blue cheese dressing for dipping.

Homemade Guacamole

Avocados are a unique fruit because they are naturally high in fat.
Since you need some fat in your diet, guacamole makes a really healthy choice.

INGREDIENTS | SERVES 4

2 ripe avocados, pitted and peeled
½ cup diced tomatoes
½ teaspoon minced fresh garlic
½ teaspoon salt
1 teaspoon finely minced green chili
1 teaspoon freshly squeezed lemon juice
½ cup fat-free sour cream (optional)

Mix all the ingredients, except sour cream, to desired texture. If the guacamole is not as creamy as you'd like, add the sour cream and serve immediately.

Celery Peanut Butter Boats

Crisp and spicy, celery is perfect with savory or slightly sweet fillings.
Celery adds fiber to anything you pile into it, and its crunch is important in snacks.

INGREDIENTS | SERVES 4

4 ribs of celery, washed or wiped clean
½ cup crunchy peanut butter
2 tablespoons toasted sesame seeds

1. Fill celery ribs with peanut butter and smooth out the top.

2. Cut the celery on the diagonal into 1" pieces.

3. Sprinkle the sesame seeds over the pieces and serve.

Never-Enough Nachos

For a quick vegetarian version, substitute 2 cups of cooked and drained black beans in place of the ground beef. You can enjoy it as a snack with friends or even as an appetizer before a meal.

INGREDIENTS | SERVES 8–10

1 pound lean ground beef
1 cup prepared salsa
1 medium tomato
4 green onions
½ cup lettuce
2 cups gluten-free tortilla chips
½ cup sour cream
1 cup shredded Cheddar cheese

1. Preheat the oven to 350°F.

2. In a large frying pan, cook the ground beef for 8–10 minutes or until it is cooked throughout. Drain the ground beef, and then place it in a large bowl.

3. Add the salsa and mix well.

4. Chop the tomato, green onions, and lettuce. Place in separate small bowls.

5. In a 2-quart casserole dish, layer the ground beef and the other ingredients in the following order, starting at the bottom:

   > Gluten-free tortilla chips
   > Ground beef-salsa mixture
   > Sour cream
   > Tomatoes
   > Green onions
   > Lettuce
   > Shredded cheese

6. Bake nachos in the preheated oven for 20–30 minutes or until the cheese is completely melted.

Mexican Quesadillas

*After trying quesadillas with just cheese, be adventurous and
add some refried beans, guacamole, or black olives.*

INGREDIENTS | SERVES 2

2 large corn tortillas
2 tablespoons shredded cheese (any type)
Sour cream or salsa (optional)

1. Place 1 tortilla on a large plate and sprinkle with the shredded cheese. Top with the second tortilla.

2. Cook in the microwave for about 20–30 seconds or until the cheese is melted.

3. Cool slightly. Use a knife or pizza cutter to cut the tortilla into 6 wedges. Dip in sour cream or salsa, as desired.

Parmesan Potato Fries

You can prepare these potatoes with or without the skin in whatever shape you like.

INGREDIENTS | SERVES 4

4 Russet potatoes
2 tablespoons oil
1 teaspoon salt
½ teaspoon pepper
1 tablespoon Parmesan cheese

1. Preheat the oven to 350°F. Line a baking pan with parchment paper.

2. Wash the potatoes. Cut them into strips, rounds, or any shape you choose.

3. Put the potatoes into a resealable bag or a large bowl. Add the oil to the bag or bowl and mix until the potatoes are well coated. Sprinkle the potatoes with salt, pepper, and Parmesan cheese. Toss again.

4. Place the potatoes in a single layer onto prepared baking pan. Bake potatoes for 45–50 minutes or until they are crispy and golden brown. Halfway through baking, flip over the potatoes so they cook evenly on all sides.

Strawberry Mango Salsa

This salsa has a sweet and spicy side to it. It is great served with grilled fish or chicken but also satisfying eaten with corn chips.

INGREDIENTS | SERVES 6

1 mango, peeled and diced
2 cups diced strawberries
1 jalapeño pepper, finely diced
¼ cup chopped cilantro
1 tablespoon balsamic vinegar
1 tablespoon lime juice

1. In a large bowl, mix together the mango, strawberries, jalapeño pepper, and cilantro.

2. Add the balsamic vinegar and lime juice, and stir to coat all the fruit with the juices.

3. Allow to chill for 30 minutes before serving. Stir again before serving.

Roasted Kale Chips

This is a simple recipe that yields a crisp, chewy kale that is irresistible. You can also slice up some collard greens or Swiss chard as a substitute for kale, or mix them all together for a tasty medley.

INGREDIENTS | SERVES 2

6 cups kale
1 tablespoon extra-virgin olive oil
1 teaspoon garlic powder

1. Preheat oven to 375°F.

2. Wash and trim kale by pulling leaves off the tough stems or running a sharp knife down the length of the stem.

3. Place leaves in a medium-size bowl and toss with extra-virgin olive oil and garlic powder.

4. Roast for 5 minutes. Turn kale over and roast another 7–10 minutes or until kale turns brown and becomes paper-thin and brittle.

5. Remove from oven and serve immediately.

Deviled Eggs

This is a quick recipe that can be whipped up in no time.
Everyone will love these and they can be easily served at parties.

INGREDIENTS | SERVES 10

10 large eggs, hard-boiled
5–6 tablespoons mayonnaise
2 green onions, finely chopped
2 cloves garlic, finely chopped
1 stalk celery, finely chopped
1 teaspoon mustard
1 teaspoon black pepper
Sweet paprika, to taste

1. Peel eggs, cut in half lengthwise, and separate yolks from whites.

2. In a large bowl, combine the egg yolks, mayonnaise, onions, garlic, celery, mustard, and black pepper. Mix well to form paste.

3. Stuff egg whites with the yolk mixture.

4. Sprinkle paprika over eggs and serve.

Edamame

Edamame are fresh soybeans. You can eat them as a snack before sushi or as part of a crudités platter.
Edamame are also an excellent addition to salads, soups, and rice dishes.

INGREDIENTS | SERVES 6

6 cups water
½ teaspoon lemon juice
1 pound frozen edamame in pods

1. In a saucepan, bring the water and the lemon juice to a boil.

2. Add the edamame and let the water come back to a boil.

3. Cook over medium-high heat for 5 minutes.

4. Drain the edamame and rinse with cold water.

5. Drain again and serve either warm or cool.

Mango Chutney

This fruity, cool chutney is a nice accompaniment to spicy dishes. To peel a ripe mango, you can slide a spoon, bottom side up, under the skin to remove it easily, without damaging the fruit.

INGREDIENTS | SERVES 8

3 mangoes

1 red onion

½ bunch fresh cilantro

1 teaspoon fresh lime juice

½ teaspoon freshly grated lime zest

Freshly ground black pepper, to taste

1. Peel and dice the mangoes and onion. Chop the cilantro.

2. Mix together all the ingredients in a medium-size bowl and adjust seasonings to taste.

CHAPTER 5

Study Snacks

Crunchy Cornbread Squares

These can also be cut into rectangles and used to scoop up yummy dips and spreads.

INGREDIENTS | MAKES 15–20 SQUARES

1 cup gluten-free cornmeal (such as Bob's Red Mill)

1 cup arrowroot starch or tapioca starch

2 teaspoons baking soda

1 teaspoon cream of tartar

1 teaspoon salt, or to taste

4 tablespoons white or brown sugar

1 cup sour cream

¼ cup buttermilk

2 eggs, beaten

4 tablespoons butter, melted

1. Prepare a 9" × 13" baking pan with nonstick spray and preheat the oven to 425°F.

2. In a large bowl, mix together the cornmeal, arrowroot starch or tapioca starch, baking soda, cream of tartar, salt, and sugar.

3. Stir in sour cream, buttermilk, eggs, and butter. (You can add various herbs and spices to change the flavors, such as oregano and garlic powder for an Italian flavor, or chili and cumin for a Mexican taste.)

4. Pour into the prepared baking pan and bake for 20 minutes or until lightly browned.

Snacking

Always a part of American eating habits, snacks should be a healthful addition to the diet. Overly sweet snacks such as cakes and candies are not all that helpful, as they produce a sugar high followed by more hunger. Real food is satisfying and keeps away hunger.

Chicken Tenders

Chicken tenders are cuts of white rib meat from the breast of a chicken.
These make a great snack when you have a crowd.

INGREDIENTS | **SERVES 4–6**

1 pound chicken tenders, cut into bite-size pieces

1 cup arrowroot starch or tapioca starch

1 teaspoon salt

Red pepper flakes, to taste

1 teaspoon baking powder

1 cup fine gluten-free cornbread crumbs

1 egg, beaten

2 tablespoons milk

Cooking oil, as needed

1. Rinse the chicken and dry on paper towels. Then lay out two sheets of waxed paper.

2. Mix together the arrowroot starch or tapioca starch, salt, pepper flakes, and baking powder and spread it on one sheet of waxed paper.

3. Spread the cornbread crumbs on the other piece of waxed paper.

4. In a small bowl, beat the egg and milk together.

5. Dredge the tenders first in the starch mixture, then in the egg mixture, and finally coat them in the crumbs.

6. In a heavy-bottomed frying pan, heat ½" of oil to 365°F and fry the chicken tenders until golden, about 3–4 minutes. Drain on paper towels.

Classic Red Tomato Salsa

Your own homemade salsa with red, ripe tomatoes tastes so much better than jarred!

INGREDIENTS | MAKES 1½–2 CUPS

6 large, ripe, juicy red tomatoes

2 cloves garlic

2 serrano or jalapeño peppers (or to taste), cored, seeded, and chopped

½ cup minced sweet white onion

Juice of 1 lime

1 teaspoon salt, or to taste

½ cup minced cilantro

Put all the ingredients in a food processor and pulse until well blended. Do not purée. Refrigerate for at least 1 hour or overnight before serving. You can vary the amount of chilies to taste.

Salsa Style

Salsa is a Mexican invention, using the hot and sweet peppers, tomatoes, herbs, and spices available. Hot food has a purpose in a hot climate: It makes you sweat, and when you sweat, you cool off—a bit. Foods that are extremely hot do kill taste buds, so don't punish your mouth.

Tropical Fruit Salsa

The sweet-hot combination is wonderful. Try it with pork, lamb, or any kind of fish.

INGREDIENTS | MAKES ABOUT 1½ CUPS

1 large mango, peeled, seeded, and diced

1 cup diced fresh pineapple

¼ cup minced red onion

1 teaspoon Tabasco sauce, or to taste

½ teaspoon freshly grated lime zest

Juice of ½ lime

Salt, to taste

Mix all the ingredients in a bowl and cover. Refrigerate for 2 hours. Serve at room temperature.

Chilies—Handle with Care

When handling chilies, it's very wise to wear rubber gloves. If they burn your mouth, they can also burn your skin. If you do not use gloves, be sure to wash your hands immediately and thoroughly after handling chilies.

Peach Salsa

This is quick and easy. Try it with cold chicken, seafood, or grilled fish.

INGREDIENTS | MAKES ABOUT 1 CUP

4 ripe peaches, peeled, seeded, and chopped

1 jalapeño pepper (or to taste), minced

Juice of 1 lime

1 teaspoon lime zest

2 tablespoons minced red onion

1 teaspoon sugar

Salt, to taste

¼ cup chopped fresh mint or parsley

Mix all ingredients together and let stand for 2 hours or in the fridge overnight. Serve at room temperature or cold.

Green Tomato (Tomatillo) Salsa

*Tomatillos are a small, green-tomato-like fruit with papery husks.
They are available in many supermarkets and all Latino markets.*

INGREDIENTS | MAKES ABOUT 1 CUP

10–12 tomatillos, husked, rinsed, and chopped

2 tablespoons olive oil

1 yellow tomato, cored and finely chopped

½ red onion, finely chopped

2 cloves garlic, minced

Juice of 1 lime and ½ teaspoon lime zest

2 serrano peppers, cored, seeded, and minced

1 teaspoon salt, or to taste

¼ cup minced parsley or cilantro

Combine all the ingredients in a bowl and cover. Let stand for 2 hours or refrigerate overnight. Serve at room temperature.

Spicy Cornbread Stuffed with Chilies and Cheese

This cornbread is perfect with soup, fried chicken, stews, and chowders, or even on its own.

INGREDIENTS | SERVES 6–8

1 cup gluten-free cornmeal (such as Bob's Red Mill, yellow or white)

1 cup brown rice flour

¼ cup light brown sugar

3 teaspoons baking powder

1 teaspoon salt

1 teaspoon red pepper flakes, or to taste

½ cup buttermilk

½ cup sour cream

2 eggs, beaten

2 tablespoons unsalted butter, melted

½ cup chopped chipotle chilies

½ cup grated pepper jack or Cheddar cheese

1. Preheat the oven to 400°F. Prepare an 8" square baking pan with nonstick spray.

2. In a large bowl, mix together the cornmeal, brown rice flour, brown sugar, baking powder, salt, and red pepper flakes.

3. Mix in buttermilk, sour cream, eggs, and melted butter.

4. Place half of the batter in the pan. Sprinkle with chilies and cheese. Cover with the rest of the batter. Bake for 20–25 minutes.

The Word on Chipotle

Chipotle chilies are jalapeño chili peppers that have been smoked and preserved in brine or vinegar. They are useful in cooking and baking, adding a smoky zing to recipes.

Winter Cranberry-Orange Cornbread

This is wonderful for breakfast, a snack, or even with turkey.
It could also be chopped and used as stuffing.

INGREDIENTS | **SERVES 8–10**

1 cup gluten-free cornmeal (such as Bob's Red Mill, yellow or white)

1 cup brown rice flour

¼ cup light brown sugar

3 teaspoons baking powder

1 teaspoon salt

1 cup milk

2 eggs, beaten

3 tablespoons unsalted butter, melted

½ cup dried cranberries

Zest of 1 orange

½ cup chopped walnuts (optional)

1. Preheat the oven to 400°F. Spray an 8" square baking pan with nonstick spray.

2. In a large bowl, mix together the cornmeal, brown rice flour, brown sugar, baking powder, and salt.

3. Slowly stir in the milk, eggs, butter, cranberries, orange zest, and walnuts, if using.

4. Turn into the pan and bake for 20–25 minutes. Cool for a few minutes before cutting into squares and serving.

Rangoon Rice Cakes

Here's an elegant party food that will make your friends think you're a culinary genius.
These cakes are spicy and go great with a nice cold cucumber salad or some chutney on the side.

INGREDIENTS | SERVES 6

6 cups cooked wild rice

½ cup minced red onion

1 clove garlic, chopped

1" fresh gingerroot, peeled and minced

1 tablespoon Madras curry powder

½ teaspoon cinnamon

2 eggs

½ cup heavy cream

1 teaspoon salt and black pepper, to taste

¼–½ cup cooking oil, as needed

2 cups gluten-free bread crumbs

½ cucumber, chopped

½ cup yogurt

Juice of ½ lemon

12 mint leaves, for garnish

1. In a large bowl, mix together the rice, onion, garlic, gingerroot, curry powder, and cinnamon.

2. Add the eggs and cream and keep mixing. Sprinkle with salt and pepper to taste and combine well.

3. Form into 12 small cakes. (The recipe can be made up to this point in advance and refrigerated for up to a day.)

4. Heat oil in a frying pan over high heat. Coat the cakes with bread crumbs and fry until golden. Place on paper towels to drain, and then on a warm platter.

5. In a small bowl, mix the cucumber, yogurt, and lemon juice and serve alongside the dish of rice cakes, with a mint leaf on top of each cake.

Rice and Wild Rice

Native Americans in the Northwest gathered wild rice in lakes. These days, basmati rice is grown in Texas. Always give wild rice extra time—it needs to grow to about six times its size to be fully cooked.

Healthy Popcorn with Yogurt

Use unbuttered popcorn and your favorite flavor of low-fat yogurt in this recipe.

INGREDIENTS | MAKES 1½ CUPS

1½ cups popped popcorn
3 tablespoons low-fat yogurt
1 tablespoon honey, warmed
¼ teaspoon nutmeg

1. Place the popcorn in a small bowl.

2. In a separate small bowl, combine the yogurt and honey.

3. Add the yogurt mixture to the popcorn, tossing to mix. Sprinkle with the nutmeg.

Low-Cal Blueberry Smoothie

The texture and tart flavor of blueberries make a nice combination with sweet banana. Enjoy as is, or add crushed ice during the final stage of blending.

INGREDIENTS | MAKES 2 CUPS

⅔ cup frozen, unsweetened blueberries
1 banana
½ cup plain, low-fat yogurt
½ cup skim milk
1 teaspoon honey

1. Wash and drain the blueberries. Peel and slice the banana.

2. Process the blueberries in a food processor or blender.

3. Add the yogurt and milk and process again.

4. Add the sliced banana and honey and process again. Serve in a tall glass.

Tropical Pineapple Smoothie

Pamper yourself by serving this smoothie in a tall, chilled glass, garnished with a wedge of lime and a few banana slices.

INGREDIENTS | MAKES 3½ CUPS

1 banana

8 ounces frozen strawberries

1 cup milk

1 cup canned crushed pineapple, with juice

2 tablespoons sweetened shredded coconut

1 teaspoon lime juice, or to taste

¼ teaspoon cinnamon, or to taste

2 crushed ice cubes

1. Peel the banana, slice, and chill in the freezer for about 15 minutes.

2. Slice the frozen strawberries.

3. Process the strawberries in a blender or food processor.

4. Add the milk and pineapple, and process again.

5. Add the banana, coconut, lime juice, cinnamon, and ice cubes, and process again. Serve in a chilled glass.

Fruity Rice Pudding

This recipe makes 2 to 3 servings. If not serving immediately, store in a sealed container in the refrigerator until ready to use. Serve cold, or warm briefly before serving.

INGREDIENTS | MAKES 3½ CUPS

1½ cups apple juice

1 cup long-grain rice

¼ teaspoon ground nutmeg

⅛ teaspoon ground allspice

½ teaspoon lemon extract

1 teaspoon vanilla extract

1 cup milk

½ cup raisins

¾ cup plain yogurt

1. In a medium-size saucepan, combine the apple juice and the rice. Stir in the nutmeg and allspice.

2. Bring the rice to a boil, uncovered, over medium heat. Cover, reduce heat, and simmer for about 20 minutes or until cooked through, stirring occasionally.

3. Remove the rice from the heat. Stir the lemon extract and vanilla extract into the milk. Then stir in the milk, followed by the raisins.

4. Whisk in the yogurt. Spoon the rice pudding into dessert dishes. Serve warm.

Roasted Pepper Medley

Letting the roasted pepper sit for several hours drains off the excess moisture.
For best results, do this whenever you want to use roasted red pepper in a salad.

INGREDIENTS | SERVES 1 OR 2

1 red bell pepper

1 orange bell pepper

3 packed cups fresh spinach leaves

2 tomatoes

1 cup canned chickpeas, drained

4 tablespoons red wine vinegar

2 teaspoons lemon juice

1 teaspoon extra-virgin olive oil

⅛ teaspoon garlic powder, or to taste

Wash Your Fruit and Vegetables!

According to a recent statistic, up to twenty strangers may have handled a tomato by the time it reaches your kitchen. That's twenty opportunities for the fruit to pick up illness-producing bacteria or germs through improper handling. Even fresh produce that is properly handled may carry dirt or pesticides. Always wash fresh fruit and vegetables in cold drinking water before eating or serving in a recipe. An added tip: Before cleaning the produce, make sure to wash your hands in soapy water so that you don't accidentally pass on unwanted germs.

1. Wash the bell peppers and pat dry. Wash the spinach leaves and drain thoroughly. Wash the tomatoes and slice.

2. Place a sheet of aluminum foil on a roasting pan. Place the peppers on the pan and broil them for 10 minutes or until the skins are blackened. Turn the peppers over after 5 minutes so that both sides blacken. Remove from oven, place in a plastic bag, and seal. Leave the peppers in the bag for at least 10 minutes.

3. After 10 minutes, remove the skin from the blackened peppers, cut them in half, and remove the seeds. Cut the peppers into long strips and let sit for 2–3 hours. Wipe the strips dry and cut into cubes.

4. In a large bowl, toss the chickpeas with the red wine vinegar, lemon juice, olive oil, and garlic powder.

5. Add the roasted pepper cubes, spinach, and sliced tomatoes and toss. Serve immediately.

Naked Fajitas

Fajitas are fun! Although onions and peppers are the most traditional sort of veggies used to make them, you can grill up any sort of produce to go with these.

INGREDIENTS | SERVES 1

1 tablespoon sliced yellow onion
1 tablespoon sliced bell pepper
2 tablespoons frozen corn
1 chicken breast, grilled
2 tablespoons shredded fat-free Cheddar cheese
1 tablespoon fat-free sour cream
1 tablespoon salsa

1. Coat a frying pan with nonstick spray. Cook the onions, peppers, and corn over medium heat for 10 minutes.

2. Slice the chicken into thin strips.

3. Add the precooked chicken to the veggies in the pan and cook for 4 minutes.

4. Place the chicken and veggies on a plate and top with Cheddar. Serve with sour cream and salsa on the side.

Pineapple Chunks in Cream Cheese

You can use fresh strawberries instead of pineapple chunks for a sweeter, less tangy treat.

INGREDIENTS | SERVES 4

1 cup canned pineapple chunks in water, drained
½ cup fat-free cream cheese, softened
⅓ cup finely chopped fresh mint

1. Dry the pineapple chunks lightly with paper towel.

2. Carefully spread the cream cheese over each pineapple chunk.

3. Roll each chunk in the chopped mint.

4. Refrigerate for 20 minutes and serve.

Fat-Free Cream Cheese

If you're used to full-fat cream cheese, the low-fat or fat-free variety will probably take some getting used to. However, once you've grown accustomed to the lighter flavor, you'll really enjoy the classic creamy texture without all the fat!

Homemade Fruit Popsicles

If you do not have an ice crusher handy at college, place the ice in a plastic bag and smash it with a hammer or other hard object to crush it before adding it to a blender. The ice is important for bulking up the mixture.

INGREDIENTS | SERVES 6

1 (12-ounce) bag frozen strawberries
3 cups 100-percent-fruit strawberry juice
1 cup crushed ice

1. Place the frozen strawberries, juice, and ice in a blender, in that order. Blend on high.

2. Pour mixture into popsicle molds.

3. Freeze for 1 hour. Remove popsicles from the freezer and insert a popsicle stick into the center of each treat. Return to the freezer and let solidify for another 7–9 hours before eating.

Popsicle Tools

If you don't have a popsicle mold, don't fret. Just use paper cups! Allow the popsicles to freeze about 1 hour, then insert popsicle sticks just as you would in the original recipe. If you don't have popsicle sticks, try plastic spoons. Anything that stays in the center of the popsicle and makes a decent handle will work.

Pineapple Coconut Smoothie

This smoothie will transplant you to the Caribbean in minutes. Garnish with a cherry and it's pure bliss.

INGREDIENTS | SERVES 1

1 cup canned unsweetened pineapple chunks
1 cup coconut water
½ cup nonfat yogurt
½ cup skim milk

Combine all the ingredients in a blender until smooth. Pour into a tall glass.

Coconut Water

Coconut water is found in young coconuts. It can be drunk straight from the coconut. Contrary to popular belief, coconut milk is not the liquid found inside a whole coconut. It is made from mixing water with shredded coconut. This mixture is strained through cheesecloth to filter out the coconut pieces.

Chewy Granola Bars

These granola bars are perfect to grab on the way out the door.
Make up a batch and you will never be stuck without something to snack on.

INGREDIENTS | SERVES 26

2 cups certified gluten-free quick-cook oats

¾ cup brown rice flour

¼ cup ground flaxseed

¼ cup slivered almonds

¼ cup uncooked quinoa

¼ cup shelled sunflower seeds

¼ cup sesame seeds

¼ cup flaked coconut

⅔ cup brown sugar

½ cup honey

4 tablespoons butter

½ teaspoon ground cinnamon

½ teaspoon salt

2 teaspoons vanilla extract

1 cup chopped dried fruit (cherries, cranberries, blueberries, apricots, etc.)

Change Things Up

Feel free to substitute for the dry ingredients, fruit, and nuts to suit your taste. Just be sure to substitute equal amounts so that the ratio of dry ingredients to syrup remains the same. If you add too many dry ingredients, the bars will not stick together. If you have too few, the bars will be overly sticky.

1. Preheat the oven to 400°F. Line a large, rimmed baking sheet with foil.

2. Mix together the oats, brown rice flour, flaxseed, almonds, quinoa, sunflower and sesame seeds, and coconut on the baking sheet. Place in the oven and toast for 10–12 minutes, stirring every few minutes to prevent burning. As soon as the oat mixture is toasted, remove the pan from the oven. While the oat mixture is toasting, line a 9" × 13" pan with parchment paper and spray lightly with cooking oil.

3. Place a small saucepan over medium-high heat and add the brown sugar, honey, butter, cinnamon, and salt. Bring the mixture to a strong boil for 2 minutes, stirring constantly. Turn off the heat and stir in vanilla.

4. Place the toasted oat mixture in a large bowl, and stir in the dried fruit. Pour the hot liquid mixture into the bowl and stir aggressively until all the ingredients are moist and well combined.

5. Using a wooden spoon, scrape the mixture onto the prepared baking sheet. Evenly spread out the mixture using a wet rubber spatula (this will help prevent sticking). Set the baking sheet aside and let the mixture cool for 2–3 hours or until it is hardened.

6. Once the mixture is hard, remove it from the pan and turn it out onto a cutting board. Remove the parchment paper. Cut the granola into bars by pressing straight down with a long knife (don't saw or they will crumble). Cut approximately 26 bars, 1" × 5½" each.

7. Wrap the bars individually in plastic wrap, and store in an airtight container at room temperature for up to a week.

Nutty Caramel Corn

A fun snack for the fall, this fan favorite is commonly seen around Halloween.
Try it along with some caramel apples, and you will have a party.

INGREDIENTS | SERVES 6

1 (3½-ounce) bag plain microwave popcorn, popped
1 cup dry-roasted, salted peanuts
1 cup brown sugar
½ cup (1 stick) butter
½ cup corn syrup or honey
¼ teaspoon salt

1. Preheat the oven to 200°F. Spray a 9" × 13" baking pan with cooking spray.

2. In a large bowl, combine the popped popcorn and nuts.

3. In a medium saucepan, combine the brown sugar, butter, corn syrup or honey, and salt. Heat over medium-high heat until mixture is melted and smooth, stirring constantly. This should take 4–5 minutes.

4. Remove the saucepan from the heat and pour caramel mixture over the popcorn and nuts, mixing well. Spread out the popcorn mixture on the prepared baking pan.

5. Bake 1 hour, stirring every 15 minutes.

Take-Along Trail Mix

Trail mix is so versatile that you can create your own versions, too. Try adding some yogurt-covered raisins, dry gluten-free cereal, candy-coated chocolate, or even popcorn.

INGREDIENTS | SERVES 4

½ cup small gluten-free pretzel sticks or twists

½ cup raisins

½ cup peanuts

¼ cup sunflower seeds

¼ cup gluten-free chocolate chips

In a large bowl, combine all the ingredients. Store in an airtight container or resealable plastic bag.

There's Gluten in That?

Always be sure to read the labels on dried fruit and nuts to ensure that the products have not come into contact with gluten during the manufacturing process.

Cinnamon-Toasted Pumpkin Seeds

This is a fun twist on the classic salted pumpkin seeds of yesteryear.

INGREDIENTS | SERVES 12

2 cups fresh pumpkin seeds
¼ cup sea salt
3 tablespoons olive oil
2 tablespoons ground cinnamon
1 teaspoon ground ginger
½ teaspoon ground cloves
¼ teaspoon ground allspice

Pumpkin Power!

Pumpkin seeds aren't just something to throw away prior to carving a jack-o'-lantern. Also known as pepitas, they are a low-calorie snack that is high in manganese, magnesium, iron, zinc, and protein. Omega-3 fatty acids, a healthy fat, are also found in pumpkin seeds.

1. Preheat the oven to 350°F. Line a baking sheet with parchment paper.

2. Place the pumpkin seeds in a large pot. Fill the pot halfway with water. Add salt. Bring to a boil. Boil for 10 minutes. Drain thoroughly.

3. Place the seeds in a medium bowl, drizzle them with olive oil, and toss to coat. Sprinkle the spices onto the seeds. Toss again to distribute the spices.

4. Arrange the seeds in a single layer on the baking sheet. Bake for 15 minutes. Turn the seeds. Bake for an additional 5 minutes or until they are toasted. Cool prior to serving.

Perfect Popcorn

High in fiber and low in fat, popcorn is the perfect whole-grain snack.

INGREDIENTS | SERVES 4

3 tablespoons oil
⅓ cup popcorn kernels

Popcorn Suggestions

Popcorn can be flavored with nearly anything! If using air-popped popcorn, a drizzle of butter will help the spices adhere. Some toppings to try are Parmesan cheese, popcorn salt and butter, chopped chives, chili powder, and lime zest.

1. Heat the oil in a 3-quart lidded saucepan. Test the temperature by tossing a few kernels in. If they pop, the oil is ready. Add the rest of the popcorn and cover. Once the popcorn starts to pop, carefully shake the pan by sliding it back and forth over the burner.

2. When the popping slows to the point that there are several seconds between pops, remove from heat and pour into a bowl. Add desired toppings.

Cinnamon Apples to Go

When you take these to go, remember to grab a napkin.
You will enjoy eating them so much, you will lick your fingers clean.

INGREDIENTS | SERVES 1

1 apple, any variety
1 teaspoon sugar
½ teaspoon cinnamon

That's a Lot of Apples!

There are more than 2,500 varieties of apples grown in the United States, and more than 100 varieties are produced commercially. On average, Americans eat about 50 pounds of apple products, per person, per year.

1. Peel the apple. Remove seeds and cut into thin slices. Place apple slices into a small resealable plastic bag.

2. Spoon the sugar and cinnamon directly into bag over apple slices.

3. Shake the bag. Take your apple slices to go.

No-Bake Honey Balls

You don't even need to run to the community kitchen to make these sweet treats!
These chewy, no-bake cookies are so easy to make, they're a good choice for beginning cooks.

INGREDIENTS | SERVES 15

½ cup honey

½ cup golden raisins

½ cup dry milk powder

1 cup crushed gluten-free crisp rice cereal

¼ cup confectioners' sugar

1 cup finely chopped dates

1 cup crushed gluten-free crisp rice cereal

Dates

Do not buy the precut dates that have been coated in sugar. They are too dry and too sweet and will upset the balance of most recipes. To chop dates, use scissors occasionally dipped into very hot water. Medjool dates, usually found in health food and gourmet stores, are richer than Deglet Noor dates.

1. In a food processor, combine the honey and raisins and process until smooth. If you don't have a food processor, simply mix the honey and raisins together in a bowl. The finished balls will have a bit chewier texture due to the raisins being left whole.

2. Scrape the mixture into a small bowl and add the milk powder, 1 cup crushed cereal, confectioners' sugar, and dates; mix well. You may need to add more sugar or honey for desired consistency.

3. Form the mixture into ¾" balls and roll in remaining crushed cereal. Store in airtight container at room temperature.

Blackberry-Yogurt Pops

These ice pops are attractive and nutritious. Blackberries are an excellent source of fiber, vitamin C, vitamin K, and folic acid.

INGREDIENTS | SERVES 6

2 cups plain yogurt
½ cup sugar
½ cup puréed blackberries

Crack the Ice Pop Code

The secret to a good ice pop is simple: sugar. Sugar lowers the freezing point of the pop so it stays soft and smooth, not brittle like an ice cube. So resist the urge to fully eliminate sugar from ice pop recipes that call for it.

1. In a medium bowl, whisk together the yogurt and sugar until the sugar dissolves. Mix in blackberries until combined.

2. Divide half of the yogurt mixture evenly between six ice pop molds. Top with remaining yogurt mixture.

3. Insert popsicle sticks and freeze until solid.

Sweetened Baby Carrots

Baby carrots are made from full-size carrots, but they're peeled and cut into smaller pieces to be more appealing. You can enjoy them raw or cooked, as in this recipe.

INGREDIENTS | SERVES 4

1 pound baby carrots
1 tablespoon butter or margarine
2 tablespoons brown sugar

1. In a large saucepan, combine the carrots and just enough water to cover them. Put the saucepan over high heat until the water begins to boil.

2. Reduce the heat to medium and continue cooking until the carrots are slightly tender, about 15 minutes.

3. Using a colander, drain the carrots and then return them to the saucepan. Add the butter or margarine and brown sugar to the saucepan, stirring until the butter is melted and the carrots are well coated.

Baked Apples

You will feel as if you're eating apple pie and your kitchen will smell like Thanksgiving dinner whenever you make this recipe.

INGREDIENTS | SERVES 6

6 Pink Lady apples
1 cup unsweetened coconut flakes
Ground cinnamon, to taste

1. Preheat the oven to 350°F.

2. Remove cores to ½" of the bottom of the apples.

3. Place apples in a medium baking dish.

4. Fill holes with coconut flakes and sprinkle with cinnamon.

5. Bake for 10–15 minutes. Apples are done when they are completely soft and brown on top.

Broccoli, Pine Nut, and Apple Salad

This quick little salad will tide you over until your next meal. The broccoli and apple taste great together, and the toasted pine nuts add a little bit of crunch.

INGREDIENTS | SERVES 2

4 tablespoons olive oil
¾ cup pine nuts
2 cups broccoli florets
2 cups diced green apple
Juice of 1 lemon

1. Heat the olive oil in a small frying pan over medium heat and sauté the pine nuts until golden brown.

2. In a medium bowl, mix the broccoli and apple together. Add the pine nuts and toss.

3. Squeeze the lemon juice over salad and serve.

Cinnamon-Toasted Butternut Squash

This side dish or snack is a great for fall. It smells amazing and will give you a carbohydrate boost that's better than any energy drink.

INGREDIENTS | SERVES 4

3 cups cubed butternut squash
1 tablespoon ground cinnamon
1 teaspoon nutmeg

1. Preheat the oven to 350°F.

2. Place the squash in a 9" × 11" baking dish. Sprinkle with cinnamon and nutmeg.

3. Bake for 30 minutes or until tender and slightly brown.

Blueberry Trail Mix

This trail mix recipe is the perfect blend of fruit and nuts to cure any hunger pangs.

INGREDIENTS | SERVES 2

¼ cup fresh or dried blueberries
¼ cup pumpkin seeds
1 ounce almonds
Dash cinnamon

Combine all the ingredients in a quart-size plastic baggie, shake, and enjoy.

Nutty Chocolate Trail Mix

*When you're craving something sweet, throw this quick trail mix together
for a healthy alternative to a chocolate bar.*

INGREDIENTS | SERVES 4

8 ounces organic, gluten-free turkey
jerky
½ cup macadamia nuts
½ cup walnuts
½ cup unsweetened coconut flakes
½ cup cacao nibs

1. Cut up the turkey jerky into bite-size pieces and place in a medium bowl.

2. Add the remaining ingredients to the bowl, mix, and serve.

Pistachio-Pumpkin Trail Mix

*This trail mix is sure to satisfy. Feel free to mix up the types of nuts
or fruits you add in to make it your own personal trail mix.*

INGREDIENTS | SERVES 4

½ cup pistachios
½ cup pumpkin seeds
½ cup sunflower seeds
½ cup coconut flakes
1 cup dried mulberries or raisins

Combine all the ingredients in a large bowl and serve.

CHAPTER 6

Microwaveable Meals

Easy Enchiladas

Preparing enchiladas in the microwave instead of baking them in the oven substantially reduces the cooking time. To speed things up even further, use leftover cooked ground beef and reheat in the microwave.

INGREDIENTS | SERVES 4

1 cup ground beef
¼ teaspoon ground cumin
¼ teaspoon salt, or to taste
⅛ teaspoon black pepper, or to taste
8 gluten-free corn tortillas
2 cups store-bought enchilada sauce
1 cup shredded Cheddar cheese

1. In a medium bowl, season the ground beef with the cumin, salt, and pepper, using your fingers to mix it in. Let the ground beef stand while you are preparing the tortillas and sauce.

2. Place the corn tortillas on a microwave-safe plate. Microwave on high heat for 30 seconds, and then for 10 seconds at a time until the tortillas look slightly dried out and are cooked.

3. Dip each of the tortillas into the enchilada sauce, letting the excess sauce drip off.

4. Using your fingers, crumble the ground beef into a 1-quart microwave-safe casserole dish. Microwave on high heat for 2 minutes. Stir and cook for another 2–3 minutes or until the ground beef is cooked through. Remove from the microwave and drain off the fat.

5. Stir ½ cup of the enchilada sauce into the meat and cook for another minute.

6. Lay a tortilla flat and spoon a portion of the meat mixture onto the lower half of the tortilla. Roll up the tortilla and place in a shallow, microwave-safe 9" × 13" baking dish. Continue with the remainder of the tortillas. Spoon leftover enchilada sauce on top. Sprinkle with the cheese.

7. Microwave on high for 5 minutes or until the cheese is melted and everything is cooked through. Let stand for 5 minutes before serving.

Frozen Garden Vegetable Soup

*Using frozen vegetables takes the work out of peeling and chopping
fresh vegetables in this quick and easy recipe.*

INGREDIENTS | SERVES 4

2 teaspoons olive oil

1 teaspoon minced garlic

1 onion, peeled and chopped

1 teaspoon dried parsley

2 cups frozen mixed vegetables

2 cups low-sodium, gluten-free beef broth

1 cup water

¼ teaspoon salt

Black pepper, to taste

½ teaspoon Tabasco sauce

1. In a medium saucepan, heat the olive oil over medium-high heat. Add the garlic and onion. Sprinkle in the dried parsley. Sauté for about 4 minutes or until the onion is softened.

2. Meanwhile, place the frozen vegetables in a microwave-safe bowl. Cook on high for about 3–4 minutes or until they are thawed and heated through.

3. Add the vegetables, beef broth, and water to the saucepan. Bring to a boil (this takes about 4 minutes). Then stir in the salt, pepper, and Tabasco sauce.

4. Turn down the heat and simmer for 3–4 minutes. Serve immediately.

Microwave Salsa Chicken

*Serve this delicious dish over couscous and topped with some
sour cream, chopped tomatoes, and diced avocado.*

INGREDIENTS | SERVES 4

1½ cups gluten-free chicken broth
2 tablespoons chili powder
½ teaspoon salt
⅛ teaspoon cayenne pepper
4 boneless, skinless chicken breasts
1 cup chunky salsa
2 tablespoons tomato paste
2 tomatoes, chopped

Tomato Paste

Tomato paste is a concentrate of fresh tomatoes, sometimes made with seasonings like basil, garlic, and oregano. You can find it in cans or in tubes. Purchase it in tubes and you can add a small amount to particular dishes without having to store leftover paste.

1. Pour the chicken broth into a microwave-safe dish. Microwave on high for 3–5 minutes or until boiling.

2. Meanwhile, sprinkle chili powder, salt, and cayenne pepper on the chicken and rub into both sides. Pierce chicken on the smooth side with a fork. Carefully place, smooth-side down, in hot chicken broth in dish.

3. Microwave the chicken on high for 8 minutes; then remove dish from oven and carefully drain off the chicken broth.

4. In small bowl, combine the salsa, tomato paste, and tomatoes and mix well.

5. Turn the chicken over, rearrange chicken in dish, and pour salsa mixture over it. Return to microwave and cook for 2–6 minutes or until chicken is thoroughly cooked, checking every 2 minutes. Let stand for 5 minutes and serve.

Microwave Chicken Divan

This method of cooking chicken breasts in the microwave yields tender, moist chicken. Serve with a spinach salad and some fresh fruit. While most jarred Alfredo sauces are gluten-free, double-check the ingredients to be sure.

INGREDIENTS | SERVES 4

1½ cups gluten-free chicken broth

½ teaspoon salt

⅛ teaspoon pepper

½ teaspoon dried thyme

4 boneless, skinless chicken breasts

1 (10-ounce) package frozen broccoli, thawed

1 (10-ounce) container refrigerated four-cheese Alfredo sauce

1 cup crushed gluten-free crackers (such as Glutino)

1. Pour the chicken broth into a microwave-safe dish. Microwave on high for 3–5 minutes or until boiling.

2. Sprinkle salt, pepper, and thyme on the chicken and rub into both sides. Pierce chicken on the smooth side with a fork. Carefully place, smooth-side down, in hot liquid in dish.

3. Microwave the chicken on high for 8 minutes, then remove dish from oven and carefully drain off the chicken broth.

4. Drain the thawed broccoli and combine in a medium bowl with the Alfredo sauce.

5. Rearrange the chicken in the dish, turning it over, and pour the broccoli mixture over the chicken. Sprinkle the top with the crushed crackers.

6. Return to the microwave and cook for 3–6 minutes or until the chicken is thoroughly cooked, checking every 2 minutes. Let stand for 5 minutes and serve.

Five-Ingredient Meatloaf

With only five ingredients to worry about in this recipe, you can get back to studying in no time.

INGREDIENTS | SERVES 4

1½ pounds ground pork

¾ cup, plus 2 tablespoons, tomato sauce

¼ cup chopped onion

1 tablespoon balsamic vinegar

½ cup Parmesan cheese

Speedy Meatloaf Muffins

Placing individual portions in muffin tins reduces baking time and makes serving easy. Better still, leftover meatloaf muffins can be frozen, making a quick and easy snack or midday meal. Bake the muffins at 350°F for 25–30 minutes or until they are cooked through.

1. In a large bowl, combine all the ingredients. When adding the tomato sauce, start with the ¾ cup and then add the remaining 2 tablespoons of sauce if more tomato flavor is desired.

2. Shape into a loaf and place in a microwave-safe casserole dish. Cover with microwave-safe wax paper.

3. Microwave on high for 15 minutes, 5 minutes at a time, rotating the dish a quarter turn between each cooking period. If the meatloaf is not cooked after 15 minutes, continue to cook for 1 minute at a time until done. (Total cooking time should be about 15 minutes.) The meatloaf is cooked when the internal temperature reaches 160°F.

4. Let stand for 5 minutes. Pour any fat off the dish and serve.

Microwave Shrimp Scampi

This dish can be multiplied to serve more people. You must proportionally increase the microwave cooking time; for example, if you double the shrimp, double the cooking time.

INGREDIENTS | SERVES 4

1 cup jasmine rice

2 cups gluten-free chicken broth

2 lemons

½ cup (1 stick) butter

1½ pounds medium raw shrimp, cleaned

¼ teaspoon garlic powder

⅛ teaspoon garlic pepper

½ teaspoon garlic salt

Quick-Cooking Rice

You don't have to use instant rice when you want some in a hurry. Read labels at the grocery store. There are some kinds of rice, including Texmati and jasmine, that cook in only 15 minutes. As a bonus, these rice varieties are fragrant and full of flavor.

1. Combine the rice and chicken broth in a medium saucepan and bring to a boil over high heat. Cover pan, lower heat to medium-low, and simmer for 15 minutes.

2. Meanwhile, zest and juice the lemons. Combine the zest, juice, and butter in a microwave-safe dish. Microwave on high for 2 minutes.

3. Sprinkle the shrimp with garlic powder, garlic pepper, and garlic salt and add to butter mixture; toss to coat shrimp. Cover and microwave on high for 2 minutes.

4. Uncover dish, stir shrimp, cover, and microwave on high for 1–3 minutes longer or until shrimp curl and turn pink.

5. Let shrimp stand, covered, for 2–3 minutes. Fluff rice with a fork. Serve shrimp and sauce over rice.

Spaghetti Squash

This squash looks like spaghetti but tastes even better!

INGREDIENTS | SERVES 3 OR 4

1 large spaghetti squash
4 tablespoons butter
3–4 tablespoons Parmesan cheese

1. Pierce the skin of the squash with a fork in five or six places and microwave for 2–3 minutes.

2. Cut the squash in half (lengthwise) and scoop out the seeds.

3. Use a fork to scrape squash into strands and place in a small serving bowl.

4. Blend squash with butter and sprinkle with Parmesan cheese. Serve immediately while still warm.

Steamed Coconut Rice

Microwave jasmine rice takes less time to make and still has the rich nutty flavor of regular boiled scented rice.

INGREDIENTS | SERVES 6

1½ cups jasmine rice

1 tablespoon butter or margarine

2 shallots, chopped

1¼ cups coconut milk

1¾ cups water

½ teaspoon salt

Or Cook It the Regular Way

Another way to cut down on the time it takes to prepare rice for dinner is to boil the rice in advance so that it just needs to be reheated. To cook basmati rice on the stovetop, sauté the butter or margarine and shallots in a frying pan until the shallots are softened. Add the rice, coconut milk, water, and salt and bring to a boil, uncovered. Turn down the heat to medium and boil, uncovered, until the liquid is nearly absorbed (10–12 minutes). Continue cooking for a few more minutes until the water is absorbed.

1. Rinse the rice in cold water and drain.

2. Place the butter or margarine and shallots in a microwave-safe 3-quart casserole dish. Microwave on high heat for 1½ minutes, stir, and then microwave for 30 seconds at a time until the shallots are tender.

3. Add the coconut milk, water, rice, and salt. Microwave on high for 10 minutes.

4. Stir the rice. Cover the dish with microwave-safe wax paper. Microwave for 3 minutes and then for 1 minute at a time until the liquid is absorbed.

5. Remove the dish from the microwave. Let stand for 5 minutes. Fluff and serve.

Easy Omelet

Don't be alarmed if the omelet has a strange shape—the egg will rise during cooking.
To prevent this from happening, cover the egg mixture tightly with plastic wrap.

INGREDIENTS | SERVES 1

2 eggs

2 tablespoons milk

Salt and pepper, to taste

1 tablespoon butter or margarine

2 slices American cheese or ¼ cup grated cheese of your choice

1. In a small bowl, lightly beat the eggs with the milk. Stir in the salt and pepper.

2. Place the butter or margarine in a microwave-safe, shallow bowl. Microwave on high for 15 seconds or until the butter melts.

3. Pour the egg mixture into the butter and stir to mix. Microwave on high for 1–2 minutes or until the egg mixture is nearly cooked.

4. Add the American cheese slices or grated cheese on top. Microwave for another 30 seconds or until the cheese melts.

Microwave Borscht

For a thicker soup, increase the amount of canned beets to 1½ cups. Like all borscht recipes, this can be served hot or cold, plain or garnished with a bit of sour cream.

INGREDIENTS | SERVES 1

1 tablespoon butter or margarine
¼ cup chopped white onion
1 cup water
2 cups gluten-free beef broth
1 cup canned beets, chopped
1 teaspoon sugar
1 teaspoon lemon juice

1. Combine the butter or margarine and the onion in a microwave-safe casserole dish. Microwave on high for 1 minute. Stir and microwave for another 1–2 minutes or until the onion is tender.

2. Add the water, beef broth, beets, sugar, and lemon juice. Microwave on high for 3 minutes. Stir and microwave for another 2–3 minutes. Serve hot or cold.

Easy Onion Soup au Gratin for One

Don't have a hot plate? This quick and easy recipe shows you how to prepare instant soup mixes in the microwave.

INGREDIENTS | SERVES 1

1½ cups water

1½ tablespoons dried onion flakes

½ teaspoon dried parsley

½ teaspoon dried onion powder

½ teaspoon sea salt

½ teaspoon celery salt

½ teaspoon turmeric

½ teaspoon sugar

½ teaspoon ground pepper

1 slice crusty gluten-free bread or toast (such as Udi's Whole Grain)

⅓ cup grated Cheddar cheese

1. Pour the water into a microwave-safe casserole dish. Stir in all of the seasonings.

2. Microwave on high for 2 minutes or until the soup is heated through.

3. Cut the bread or toast into several cubes. Add the cubes to the dish and sprinkle the grated cheese on top. Microwave on high for 3 more minutes or until the cheese melts.

Microwave Green Beans

The trick to this recipe is making sure the green beans are covered with the broth.
This recipe also works well with fresh snow peas—be sure to trim the ends before cooking.

INGREDIENTS | SERVES 1 OR 2

3½ ounces fresh green beans
⅓ cup gluten-free chicken broth

1. Rinse the green beans under cold, running water. Drain and pat dry.

2. Place the green beans in a microwave-safe bowl and cover with the chicken broth. Cook on high heat for 1½–2 minutes or until they are crisp and bright green.

3. Serve with butter, margarine, or gluten-free soy sauce if desired.

Fruity Snow Peas

Canned fruit cocktail juice adds a sweet flavor to delicate snow peas.

INGREDIENTS | SERVES 2–3

6 ounces fresh snow peas

½ cup canned fruit cocktail juice

Are Your Dishes Microwave-Safe?

There is an easy way to find out if your dishes are microwave-safe. Fill the dish with water and microwave on high. If the water heats up and the dish remains at room temperature, it is safe to use.

1. Rinse the snow peas under cold, running water. Drain and pat dry. Trim the ends.

2. Place the snow peas in a shallow, microwave-safe bowl and add the fruit cocktail juice. Cook on high for 1½–2 minutes or until the snow peas are crisp and bright green.

Corn on the Cob

The microwave gives a quick and easy alternative to boiling corn in a large pot of water. If cooking two ears of corn at once, increase the cooking time to 4–5 minutes.

INGREDIENTS | SERVES 1

1 ear corn

1. Remove the husk from the corn. Wrap the corn in microwave-safe wax paper and place on a paper towel or microwave-safe dish.

2. Microwave on high heat for 2–3 minutes. Let stand in microwave for a few minutes. Serve with salt and butter if desired.

Baked Potato

Want a bit of melted butter with your baked potato? Slice it open, add 1 tablespoon of butter, and place the potato back into the microwave for about 30 seconds.

INGREDIENTS | SERVES 1

1 baking potato

Potato Cooking Times

The time it takes to cook a potato in the microwave can vary quite a bit, depending on the size of the potato and the strength of your microwave. To be safe, cook the potato on high for 3 minutes, check it with a fork, and then continue cooking in 2-minute increments as needed. The potato is cooked when it is tender and can easily be pierced with a fork. The skin may also be slightly wrinkled.

1. Wash the potato, scrubbing off any dirt. Pierce the potato in several spots with a fork.

2. Place the potato on a paper plate or microwave-safe plate and cook on high for 3–7 minutes or until cooked through (the internal temperature should be 210°F).

3. Slice the potato open and add your toppings of choice.

Stuffed Potato

For a little variety, feel free to add your own favorite ingredients to the potato stuffing.

INGREDIENTS | SERVES 1

1 large baking potato (about 8 ounces)
2 tablespoons sour cream
1 tablespoon butter or margarine
¼ teaspoon paprika
¼ teaspoon salt
Pepper, to taste
2 teaspoons shredded Cheddar cheese

How Does a Microwave Work?

Microwaves, which operate within the same frequency as radio waves, bounce off the metal walls of the oven. When the microwaves hit the food, they cause the water molecules in the food to vibrate. This in turn produces the heat that cooks the food. All microwave ovens have two safety systems to ensure that the microwaves stop moving the moment the oven door is opened so that no radiation escapes into the room.

1. Wash the potato, scrubbing off any dirt. Pierce the potato in several spots with a fork.

2. Place the potato on a paper plate or microwave-safe plate and cook on high for 3–7 minutes or until cooked through. Let the potato sit for about 1 minute before removing from the microwave.

3. Slice the potato open. Carefully scoop out most of the potato, leaving about ¼" pulp around the skin.

4. Mash the potato pulp with the sour cream, butter or margarine, paprika, salt, and pepper. Sprinkle the shredded cheese on top.

5. Spoon the mixture into the potato shell and microwave for 3–5 minutes or until the cheese melts.

Teriyaki Chicken

White wine vinegar makes a convenient substitute for Japanese mirin in this recipe.
You can use mirin, saké, or any other type of rice wine in this recipe;
just double-check the ingredients to make sure they are gluten-free.

INGREDIENTS | SERVES 1

1 (6-ounce) boneless, skinless chicken breast

¼ cup gluten-free soy sauce (such as La Choy)

¼ cup white wine vinegar

1 tablespoon sugar

1. Rinse the chicken breast under running water and pat dry. Cut into bite-size pieces.

2. In a small bowl, mix together the soy sauce, white wine vinegar, and sugar.

3. Place the chicken breast in a microwave-safe glass baking dish. Pour the sauce over the chicken. Cover with plastic wrap.

4. Microwave the chicken on high for 3 minutes. Turn the chicken over and microwave for 2–3 more minutes, checking every 30 seconds during the last minute of cooking to see if it is done.

Garlic Chicken

That's right, a delicious chicken dinner from the microwave! If your microwave is large enough, feel free to microwave the garlic butter with the chicken during the last 30 seconds of cooking.

INGREDIENTS | SERVES 1

2 cloves garlic

1 (6-ounce) boneless, skinless chicken breast

1½ teaspoons olive oil

1 teaspoon dried oregano

¼ cup chopped onion

3 tablespoons butter or margarine, divided

Speedy Reheating in the Microwave

A microwave provides a quick alternative to reheating food on the stovetop. To reheat, spread out the food on a microwave-safe dish, arranging it so that the thicker or meatier sections are on the outside. For meat or other dry foods, add a bit of liquid to speed up cooking. Use the reheat setting if your microwave has one. If not, cook on high for 2–3 minutes.

1. Smash, peel, and chop the garlic cloves. Rinse the chicken breast under cold, running water and pat dry. Use a pastry brush to brush the olive oil over the chicken. Rub the dried oregano on both sides of the breast.

2. Place the chicken breast in a microwave-safe bowl and cover with plastic wrap. Microwave on high for 3 minutes. Turn the chicken over and microwave on high for 3 more minutes or until the chicken is cooked through. Set aside.

3. Place the onion and 2 tablespoons of the butter or margarine in a microwave-safe bowl. Microwave on high for 1 minute. Stir and then microwave for 30 seconds.

4. Stir in the garlic and the remaining 1 tablespoon butter or margarine. Microwave for 1–1½ minutes or until the onion is tender and the garlic aromatic.

5. Pour the garlic butter over the chicken.

Easy "Tandoori" Chicken

This takes some planning ahead, since the chicken must marinate overnight.
Curry powder takes the place of a garam masala spice mixture in this quick and easy microwave dish.
Canned or fresh pineapple juice can be substituted for the coconut milk.

INGREDIENTS | SERVES 2

2 (7-ounce) boneless, skinless chicken breasts

1 teaspoon curry powder, or to taste

2 teaspoons lemon juice

¼ cup plain yogurt

½ cup coconut milk

1. Rinse the chicken breasts under cold, running water and pat dry with paper towels.

2. Cut four diagonal slits on the top side of each chicken breast, being careful not to cut completely through the meat. Turn the breasts over and make two to three diagonal cuts, again being careful not to cut completely through the meat.

3. In a small bowl, mix the curry powder and lemon juice into the yogurt.

4. Rub the yogurt mixture thoroughly over the chicken breasts so that the yogurt fills the cut areas. Place the breasts in a bowl or plastic container, seal or cover with plastic wrap, and refrigerate overnight.

5. Remove the marinated chicken from the refrigerator and cut into cubes. Place the chicken cubes in a microwave-safe casserole dish. Add the coconut milk. Cover the dish with plastic wrap. Microwave on high for 5 minutes.

6. Uncover the chicken and microwave for 1–3 more minutes or until the chicken breasts are cooked but still tender.

Chili

Frozen ground beef can be defrosted in the microwave. Remove the ground beef from the package, place on a microwave-safe plate, and defrost according to the manufacturer's instructions on your microwave. Cook the ground beef immediately after thawing.

INGREDIENTS | SERVES 1 OR 2

1 tablespoon olive oil or margarine
¼ onion, chopped
½ green bell pepper, chopped
½ pound ground beef
½ tablespoon chili powder, or to taste
½ tablespoon brown sugar
1 cup canned chickpeas, with liquid
½ cup canned green beans, with liquid
1½ cups tomato sauce

1. Place the olive oil or margarine and onion in a shallow 2-quart microwave-safe casserole dish. Microwave on high for 1 minute.

2. Add the green pepper and microwave on high for 1 more minute or until the onion is tender.

3. Stir in the ground beef. Microwave on high for 5 minutes. Stir and cook for 3–4 minutes or until the meat is thoroughly browned. Remove from the microwave and drain the fat from the ground beef.

4. Stir in the chili powder and brown sugar. Microwave on high for 1 minute.

5. Stir in the chickpeas, green beans, and tomato sauce. Microwave on high for 10–15 minutes or until the chili has thickened. Make sure the ground beef is cooked through. Enjoy hot.

Pork with Italian Seasonings

For a quick and easy dinner, serve the pork with canned chickpeas or leftover hummus dip.
The flavor of the chickpeas goes nicely with pork.

INGREDIENTS | SERVES 1

½ pound pork tenderloin

¼ teaspoon dried basil, or to taste

¼ teaspoon dried parsley, or to taste

¼ cup chopped onion (optional)

1 tablespoon butter or margarine (optional)

1 cup gluten-free creamy mushroom soup (such as Progresso Creamy Mushroom Soup)

1. Rinse the pork and pat dry. Rub the basil and parsley over the pork. Cut it into cubes.

2. If using the onion and butter or margarine, combine in a microwave-safe casserole dish. Microwave on high for 1 minute. Stir and microwave for another 1–2 minutes or until the onion is tender.

3. Add the pork cubes and soup. Cover with plastic wrap and microwave on high for 4 minutes. Rotate the dish. Microwave on high for 2–3 more minutes or until the pork is cooked. (The pork is done when it feels firm when pressed and the juices run clear when poked with a fork.)

Fast Mocha Fudge

*Don't slice the bars too thickly. This recipe makes a very sweet fudge
with a strong mocha flavor—a little goes a long way.*

INGREDIENTS | MAKES ABOUT 24 BARS

2¼ cups sugar

¾ cup semisweet chocolate chips

½ cup (1 stick) butter or margarine

½ cup sweetened condensed milk

¼ cup brewed coffee

¼ cup gluten-free instant hot chocolate
mix (most brands are gluten-free, but
always remember to double-check)

½ cup walnut pieces

1. Grease an 8" × 8" baking pan.

2. Combine the sugar, chocolate chips, butter or margarine, milk, coffee, and instant hot chocolate mix in a microwave-safe bowl. Microwave on high for 3 minutes. Stir and microwave on high for 1-minute intervals, stirring each time, until the butter and chocolate are melted.

3. Pour the mixture into the prepared baking pan. Stir in the walnuts. Cover and refrigerate until it has set. Slice into 2" squares.

CHAPTER 7

Easy Main Dishes

Savory Rice and Sausage

This is so easy and really great for any time when you are in a rush to get to class.

The Old-Fashioned Ways

Once seasoned, a heavy cast-iron frying pan will last for generations. In fact, they never wear out. And being of such thick metal, they distribute heat evenly. Seasoning the pan requires just a skim of oil left on a warm pan overnight. Then, don't overuse detergent when cleaning.

1. Brown the sausage pieces, onion, and garlic for about 8–10 minutes. If the sausage is very lean, add a bit of olive oil to prevent the food from sticking.

2. Stir in the rice and toss with the sausage and vegetables. Add the broth and rosemary and cover. In a broiler-safe frying pan or casserole dish, cook on very low heat or place in a 325°F oven for 45–60 minutes, depending on the type of rice you are using. (Do not use Minute Rice.)

3. Just before serving, sprinkle the top with Parmesan cheese and brown under the broiler. Add the parsley and serve.

Scalloped Potatoes with Leeks and Country Ham

*This is a great brunch or supper dish. It's filling and delicious,
and especially good on a cold day or nippy evening.*

INGREDIENTS | SERVES 6

4 tablespoons butter (for greasing baking dish and dotting on potatoes)

1½ cups grated Parmesan cheese

1 cup coarsely grated fontina cheese

½ cup brown rice flour

Salt and freshly ground black pepper, to taste

6 Idaho or Yukon Gold potatoes, peeled and thinly sliced

4 leeks, thinly sliced crosswise, white parts only

1 pound deli ham, diced

3 cups milk

1. Grease a baking dish with butter or prepare it with nonstick spray. Preheat oven to 350°F.

2. Mix together the cheeses, brown rice flour, and salt and pepper.

3. Place a layer of potatoes in the baking dish, then one of leeks, and dab with bits of ham. Sprinkle with the cheese-flour mixture. Repeat until you get to the top of the baking dish. Add the milk, sprinkle with remaining cheese mixture, and dot with butter.

4. Bake for about 90 minutes. The top should be brown and crispy, and the inside soft and creamy.

Tuscan Bean, Tomato, and Parmesan Casserole

*When you want to whip up something satisfying, warming,
and delicious for a long study session, this is it!*

INGREDIENTS | SERVES 4–6

4 slices bacon

¼ cup olive oil

4 cloves garlic, coarsely chopped

1 medium onion, peeled and coarsely chopped

½ fresh fennel bulb, coarsely chopped, or thinly sliced green cabbage

1 tablespoon brown rice flour

2 cans white beans, drained and rinsed

16 ounces tomatoes, chopped (canned is fine)

1 medium zucchini, chopped

1 tablespoon chopped fresh basil

1 teaspoon dried oregano

½ cup rinsed and chopped fresh Italian parsley

1 teaspoon red pepper flakes, or to taste

1 teaspoon salt, or to taste

½ cup freshly grated Parmesan cheese

2 tablespoons unsalted butter, cut into small pieces

1. Fry the bacon until almost crisp. Drain on paper towels, chop, and set aside. Remove all but 1 teaspoon of bacon fat from frying pan. Add the oil, garlic, onion, and fennel or green cabbage. Sauté over low heat for 10 minutes or until softened but not browned.

2. Preheat oven to 350°F. Blend the brown rice flour into the mixture and cook for 3 minutes.

3. Add the beans, tomatoes, and zucchini. Mix well and pour into a casserole dish. Add the herbs, red pepper flakes, and salt. Stirring, mix in the reserved chopped bacon.

4. Sprinkle Parmesan cheese and butter over the top and bake for 25 minutes or until the cheese is lightly browned.

Eat More Beans

There are more varieties of legumes than it's possible to list here. They are delicious and loaded with protein, vitamins, minerals, and fiber. If you need to stretch your food supply, beans are the answer. They come in red and pink, green and orange, black and white, speckled or solid. Some have black eyes and others look like cranberries. Beans—legumes—are available in many sizes and shapes, from tiny peas to big kidneys.

Turkey and Fruit

*Vary the flavors in this dish by adding fresh sage or fresh parsley.
You can also substitute a variety of mushrooms for the fruit.*

INGREDIENTS | SERVES 4

2 tablespoons butter

½ cup chopped sweet onion

2 stalks celery, rinsed and chopped

2 tart apples, peeled, cored, and chopped

2 ripe pears, peeled, cored, and chopped

½ cup dried cranberries

1 teaspoon dried thyme

2 teaspoons crumbled dried rosemary

1¼ pounds sliced fresh turkey breast or thigh

Salt and pepper, to taste

½ cup apple cider

½ cup gluten-free chicken broth

1½ cups gluten-free cornbread crumbs

1. Melt the butter and add the onion and celery. Sauté until soft, about 10 minutes, over low heat. Add the fruit and herbs. Cook until just tender, about 5 more minutes.

2. Preheat oven to 350°F.

3. Prepare a baking dish with nonstick spray. Sprinkle the turkey with salt and pepper and place it in the baking dish. Spread it with the fruit mixture.

4. Add the cider and broth. Sprinkle the top with cornbread crumbs. Bake for 45 minutes.

Serving Suggestion—Serve with Rice

More varieties of rice are now on the market. It used to be just Uncle Ben's and Carolina. Today, you can buy Arborio rice from Italy and basmati rice, the staple of the Indian and Chinese diets. You can also buy purple rice, brown rice, and sticky rice. Arborio and basmati rice are short-grained and stubby. They contain more starch and therefore make a lot more "cream" than other varieties do when cooked. Try them all and you will find favorites. Basmati and Arborio varieties are wonderful in risotto, baked rice, and rice pudding.

Zucchini with Seafood, Tomato, and Bacon

*This recipe can use baseball-bat-size zucchinis, but it's better
with the medium ones, about 10–12 inches each.*

INGREDIENTS | SERVES 6 ·

6 medium zucchinis

1 small onion, peeled and minced

2 cloves garlic, peeled and minced

1 serrano pepper, cored, seeded, and minced

2 tablespoons butter or olive oil

1 cup cooked rice

1 cup crushed tomatoes

1 pound crabmeat

2 tablespoons freshly squeezed lemon juice

2 eggs

1 tablespoon dried oregano, or 2 tablespoons fresh oregano

Salt and pepper, to taste

6 strips bacon, for garnish

1. Cut the top quarter off of the zucchinis, lengthwise. Hollow out the zucchinis with the small side of a melon baller or with a ½-teaspoon measuring spoon; reserve pulp.

2. Sauté the onion, garlic, pepper, and zucchini pulp in the butter or olive oil until soft. Add all remaining ingredients except the bacon.

3. Preheat the oven to 350°F.

4. Divide the filling among the zucchini "boats." Lay a bacon strip on top of each stuffed zucchini. Place in a baking dish prepared with nonstick spray or oil. Bake until the "boats" are hot and the bacon is brown and crisp. Serve hot or at room temperature.

Stuffed Vegetables

There are many vegetables you can successfully stuff with lots of different delicious ingredients. Chopped meat, shrimp, fish, and crabmeat make wonderful stuffings. A baked clam-stuffed mushroom is also a real treat. Ricotta cheese, used to stuff pastas such as ravioli and lasagna, also makes an excellent stuffing.

Crispy Potato-Crusted Chicken

When you use this crust on your baked chicken, you'll find it's really crispy and crunchy. Don't add salt, as the potato chips are already salty.

INGREDIENTS | SERVES 4

12 ounces gluten-free potato chips
4 boneless, skinless chicken breasts
⅔ cup sour cream
1 teaspoon freshly ground black pepper
2 tablespoons snipped fresh chives
1 teaspoon dried thyme

1. In a food processor, chop up potato chips until you have 1 cup of crumbs.

2. Rinse the chicken, dry on paper towels, and lay it in a baking dish prepared with nonstick spray.

3. Preheat the oven to 350°F. Spread the chicken with sour cream. Combine the potato-chip crumbs with the pepper, chives, and thyme and sprinkle mixture over chicken. Bake for 25 minutes or until brown and crispy.

Old-Fashioned Chicken Cacciatore with Spaghetti Squash

You can vary this dish by adding fresh mint, capers,
and lemon zest, and by using red vermouth rather than red wine.

INGREDIENTS | SERVES 4–6

1 (3½-pound) chicken, cut into 8 pieces

1 cup brown rice flour

Salt and pepper, to taste

1 teaspoon fresh oregano

¼ cup olive oil

1 teaspoon butter

1 onion, peeled and diced

2 or 3 cloves garlic, peeled and minced

2 tablespoons fresh rosemary

2 cups mushrooms, wiped clean and chopped

1 (16-ounce) jar gluten-free marinara sauce, or 16 ounces canned tomatoes

4 ounces dry red table wine, or to taste

½ cup Parmesan cheese

1 bunch fresh parsley, chopped, for garnish

1. Dredge the chicken in the brown rice flour, salt and pepper, and oregano. Heat the oil and butter together until butter melts. Sauté chicken in the oil-and-butter mixture. Add the onion, garlic, rosemary, and mushrooms. Sauté for 5 minutes.

2. Add the tomato sauce or tomatoes and red wine. Cover and simmer over very low heat for 1 hour. Remove cover, place chicken on a platter, and continue to simmer sauce until reduced by half.

3. Spoon sauce over the chicken and sprinkle with cheese and parsley.

Tenderloin of Pork with Spinach and Water Chestnuts

For convenience, use fresh baby spinach, prewashed and packed in a bag. Serve this dish with rice.

INGREDIENTS | SERVES 4

2 pork tenderloins, about ¾ pound each

¼ cup brown rice flour

¼ teaspoon nutmeg

¼ teaspoon ground cloves

Salt and pepper, to taste

¼ cup olive oil

2 tablespoons lemon juice

1 teaspoon gluten-free Worcestershire sauce

1 (8-ounce) bag fresh baby spinach or 1 (10-ounce) box frozen chopped spinach, thawed

½ cup sliced water chestnuts

1. Trim the pork and cut into serving pieces. On a sheet of waxed paper, mix together the brown rice flour and seasonings. Dredge the pork in the flour mixture.

2. Sauté the pork in the olive oil for about 6 minutes per side, or until the juices run clear when a knife is inserted into the middle of each piece of meat. Remove from pan and keep warm.

3. Add the lemon juice, Worcestershire sauce, spinach, and water chestnuts to the pan. Stir to wilt spinach. Serve wilted vegetables and sauce over cooked pork.

Buying Pork

While you can get "heirloom" or "heritage" pork varieties online, you can buy a basic pork tenderloin in almost any supermarket. Tenderloin is one of the best and most juicy cuts of pork available.

Spicy Mixed Meatballs

Meatballs generally have bread as a filler and outside coating, but in this recipe you'll use ground potato chips. The eggs hold the balls together, and the ground chips taste wonderful and help to create a moist and flavorful meatball.

INGREDIENTS | MAKES 10–12 MEATBALLS

1 pound meatloaf mix—ground beef, pork, and veal

2 eggs

2 cloves garlic, minced

1 teaspoon dried oregano

½ teaspoon cinnamon

½ teaspoon fennel seeds

½ cup finely grated Parmesan cheese

Salt and pepper, to taste

2 cups crushed low-salt, gluten-free potato chips, divided

Light oil, such as canola, for frying

1. In a large bowl, mix all ingredients except 1 cup of the crushed potato chips and the cooking oil.

2. Place a large sheet of waxed paper on the counter. Sprinkle remaining cup of chip crumbs on it.

3. Form meat mixture into balls, roll in crumbs, and fry them in oil until well browned (about 5–7 minutes). Drain on paper towels and then refrigerate, freeze, or serve with the marinara sauce of your choice.

Spicy Meatballs

You can add spice to your meatballs by grinding up some hot Italian sausage and mixing it with the ground meat you're using. A truly great Italian sausage has aromatics like garlic, and herbs and spices such as anise seeds.

Maryland-Style Crab Cakes with Country Ham

*The addition of country ham balances the sweetness
of the crabmeat and gives the whole thing a great lift.*

INGREDIENTS | MAKES 8 CRAB CAKES

½ cup mayonnaise

2 eggs

1 teaspoon Dijon-style mustard

1 teaspoon gluten-free Worcestershire sauce

Salt, to taste

1 teaspoon red pepper flakes, or to taste

1 tablespoon fresh lemon juice

1 cup gluten-free cornbread crumbs, divided

1¼ pounds lump blue crabmeat

Oil for frying

Lemon wedges, for garnish

1. In a large bowl, mix the mayonnaise, eggs, mustard, Worcestershire sauce, salt, pepper flakes, and lemon juice. Stir until well mixed.

2. Add half the cornbread crumbs and gently toss in the crabmeat. Form 8 cakes and coat with more cornbread crumbs.

3. Over medium heat, bring the oil to 300°F. Fry the cakes, turning after 5 minutes, until golden brown. Serve with lemon wedges.

Topping Off Crab Cakes

Some cooks add finely chopped onion to their crab cake mixture. Others use chives. You can also add finely chopped parsley. Some like their crab cakes with tartar sauce, others with cocktail sauce. Use the flavors you enjoy most!

Codfish Broiled on a Bed of Paper-Thin Potatoes

Cod is one of the world's most beloved and versatile fish.
It can be baked, broiled, steamed, poached, salted, or cooked with milk in a stew.

INGREDIENTS | SERVES 4

2 pounds Idaho or Yukon Gold potatoes, peeled and sliced paper-thin

¼ cup olive oil

2 tablespoons butter, melted

Salt and pepper, to taste

4 cod fillets or steaks, about 5 ounces each

Salt and pepper, for the fish

Butter, for the fish

Chopped parsley, for garnish

Lemon wedges, for garnish

Crabmeat

There is a lot of crab and fake crabmeat around. The very best is Maryland blue crab, in lumps or flakes; it's also the most expensive, running up to $15 a pound. Fake crab, or surimi, is made from fish that has been cooked with the water and juices from crabmeat; it is cheap and it generally has wheat as a filler ingredient. Blue crabs are rounded and squat with short legs, unlike the gigantic, spider-like legs of Alaskan king crab or the finger-like clusters of snow crab. There's nothing like a good fresh crab, whether from Alaska or Maryland.

1. Preheat the oven to 400°F.

2. In a baking pan prepared with nonstick spray, toss the potatoes with oil, butter, and salt and pepper.

3. Bake the potatoes for 40 minutes or until the top is brown and crisp and the inside soft.

4. When the potatoes are done, lay the fish on top, sprinkle with salt and pepper, dot with butter, and reheat the oven to broil.

5. Broil until the fish is done, about 8–10 minutes, depending on the thickness of the fish. If the potatoes start to burn, move the pan to a lower rack in the oven.

6. Sprinkle with parsley and serve with lemon wedges.

Thick and Creamy Corn and Lima Bean Casserole

You can also add some chopped ham to this dish to give it both extra flavor and protein.

INGREDIENTS | SERVES 4 OR 5

2 tablespoons unsalted butter

½ sweet onion, finely chopped

½ cup minced celery

½ cup minced celery root

¼ cup chopped roasted red pepper

2 tablespoons brown rice flour

½ cup gluten-free chicken broth

1 (10-ounce) package frozen lima beans

1 (10-ounce) package frozen corn kernels

2 eggs, well beaten

1½ cups whipping cream

1 teaspoon salt

1 teaspoon sweet paprika

1 teaspoon ground black pepper

1 teaspoon ground coriander

½ teaspoon ground allspice

1 cup gluten-free bread crumbs

1 cup grated Cheddar cheese

Better Than Canned

While some brands of creamed corn are gluten-free, not all are. It's often easier to stick with fresh or frozen corn, making your own cream sauce. It's easy, naturally gluten-free, and tastes so much better than the ones made with soups or mixes.

1. Preheat the oven to 350°F. Melt the butter in a large, ovenproof casserole dish. Add the onion, celery, celery root, and red pepper; sauté over low heat until soft, about 10 minutes.

2. Mix in the brown rice flour and stir, cooking gently for 3 minutes.

3. Add the chicken broth, lima beans, and corn. Bring to a boil and then lower the heat to a simmer and cook until the lima beans are slightly softened, about 20 minutes.

4. Take off the heat. Mix together the eggs and cream; blend quickly into the vegetables. Mix in the salt and spices. Place in a well-buttered casserole dish or keep in the same ovenproof pan that you've been using. Sprinkle the top with bread crumbs and cheese.

5. Bake until golden brown and bubbling, about 20 minutes. Serve hot.

Sesame-Crusted Chicken Breasts

*Serve this with rice and lots of vegetables. Leftovers can be chopped,
mixed with a spicy sauce, and eaten with gluten-free chips as a tasty snack.*

INGREDIENTS | SERVES 4

¼ cup pineapple juice

¼ cup orange juice

1 tablespoon lime juice

½ cup gluten-free soy sauce (such as La Choy)

1" gingerroot, peeled and minced

2 cloves garlic (or to taste), minced

1 teaspoon chili oil, or to taste

2 large boneless, skinless chicken breasts, halved

1 egg, beaten

½ cup sesame seeds

1. In a nonreactive bowl or glass pan large enough to hold the chicken, whisk together the juices, soy sauce, ginger, garlic, and chili oil.

2. Rinse the chicken breasts and pat dry with paper towels. Add the chicken to the sauce and turn to coat. Cover and refrigerate for 4 hours.

3. Drain the chicken; dip in beaten egg and then in sesame seeds. Grill or sauté in oil for 6 minutes per side, depending on thickness of meat. Serve hot.

Chili and Other Hot Sauces

Chinese, Indians, and other groups in Asia, Southeast Asia, and Asia Minor make their own versions of chili for cooking. Chili oil is extremely hot. Chili paste comes in green and red and is popular in Thailand. The Chinese make a chili-and-garlic paste that is called Sichuan chili. Tabasco sauce, fresh chopped chilies (red and/or green), cayenne pepper, and red pepper flakes can be substituted.

Unstuffed Cabbage Roll Casserole

Don't feel like rolling up cabbage leaves? This recipe gives the taste of cabbage rolls without the work.

INGREDIENTS | SERVES 4

1 head green cabbage
2 tablespoons butter or margarine
1 pound ground beef
½ onion, chopped
Salt and pepper, to taste
1½ cups cooked brown rice
2 cups tomato sauce
4 tablespoons white vinegar
4 teaspoons sugar

Cabbage—a Nutritional Powerhouse

Nutritionists believe that cabbage—particularly raw cabbage—is one of the healthiest vegetables. Besides being rich in vitamin C, cabbage contains vitamin A, vitamin E, calcium, and folic acid. To gain the greatest nutritional value from cabbage, enjoy it raw. Dieters, have no fear—1 cup of shredded cabbage contains less than 25 calories.

1. Preheat the oven to 325°F.

2. Boil the cabbage in a large pot of salted water. Drain and chop into pieces to yield approximately 3 cups.

3. Heat the butter or margarine in a frying pan over medium heat. Add the ground beef. When the beef is nearly cooked through, add the onion. Continue cooking until the onion is tender, about 5 minutes. Drain the excess fat from the pan.

4. Stir in the salt and pepper, rice, tomato sauce, white vinegar, and sugar. Cook for a few minutes to heat through.

5. Line the bottom of a casserole dish with the chopped cabbage. Pour the ground beef mixture on top. Bake for 1–1½ hours, until the cabbage is tender.

Chicken with Marinated Artichoke Hearts

Prepare the artichoke hearts a day in advance. You could also substitute boiled potatoes for the cooked rice. Chop the boiled potatoes into chunks and add to the frying pan during the final stages of cooking.

INGREDIENTS | SERVES 1 OR 2

2 (5-ounce) boneless chicken thighs

⅛ teaspoon salt

⅛ teaspoon pepper

1 recipe Marinated Artichoke Hearts (see Chapter 3)

⅓ cup gluten-free chicken broth

¼ cup tomato sauce

2 teaspoons sugar

1 cup cooked rice or gluten-free pasta

1. Rinse the chicken thighs and pat dry. Remove the skin and any excess fat. Rub the salt and pepper over the chicken.

2. Heat 2 tablespoons of the olive oil marinade from the Marinated Artichoke Hearts in a deep frying pan over medium heat. Add the chicken thighs and cook until browned on both sides.

3. Drain any excess fat out of the frying pan. Add the chicken broth, tomato sauce, sugar, and the Marinated Artichoke Hearts (including the tomatoes and marinade). Cover and simmer for 15 minutes. Make sure the chicken thighs are fully cooked through. Serve with the cooked rice or pasta.

Basic Steamed Chicken with Carrots

*An electric steaming unit makes a nutritious and easy-to-use alternative to a stove.
If your college doesn't allow you to keep one in your dorm room,
ask if you can keep it in your dorm's communal kitchen instead.*

INGREDIENTS | SERVES 2

2 (5-ounce) boneless, skinless chicken breasts

½ cup baby carrots

1 tablespoon fresh rosemary

⅛ teaspoon salt, or to taste

⅛ teaspoon freshly ground black pepper

1. Rinse the chicken breasts and pat dry. Cut off any excess fat. Wash the baby carrots and dry. Leave whole or cut in half.

2. Lay the chicken breasts flat in the top part of the steamer. If your steaming unit has a screen for herbs, lay the rosemary on it. If not, lay the rosemary around the chicken breasts.

3. Set the steaming unit's timer according to the manufacturer's instructions. After the chicken has been steaming for 5 minutes, open the lid and add the baby carrots. Steam until the chicken is cooked through and the carrots are tender. (The exact time will vary according to the steaming model, but boneless chicken is normally steamed for 20–25 minutes, and carrots for 15–20 minutes.) Add salt and pepper and serve.

Three-Bean Cassoulet

To make a more filling dish, cut up two or three leftover cooked sausages and stir them into the cassoulet during the final 15 minutes of cooking.

INGREDIENTS | SERVES 1 OR 2

1 clove garlic

4 ounces fresh snap beans or other green beans

1 zucchini

⅓ cup chopped white onion

1 cup Romano beans (also called Italian flat beans)

¾ cup black-eyed peas

1 cup tomato sauce

1 cup gluten-free chicken broth or water

1 teaspoon dried parsley

½ teaspoon dried basil

⅛ teaspoon salt, or to taste

Having Fun with Gluten-Free Pasta

Tired of spaghetti or linguine? Pasta comes in a number of intriguing shapes and sizes. For example, fusilli are shaped like short "springs," while gnocchi resemble stuffed shells. And then there are tube-shaped pastas, such as penne, manicotti, and rigatoni. The next time you have a yen for pasta, try experimenting with different types; just make sure they are gluten-free.

1. Preheat oven to 350°F.

2. Smash, peel, and chop the garlic clove. Wash the snap beans and drain. Trim the ends and cut off any brown spots. Wash, peel, and slice the zucchini.

3. Bring a pot of water to a boil. Blanch the snap beans in the boiling water for about 3 minutes or until they turn bright green.

4. In an ungreased 1½- or 2-quart casserole dish, combine the garlic, snap beans, zucchini, onion, Romano beans, black-eyed peas, tomato sauce, and chicken broth or water. Stir in the dried parsley, dried basil, and salt.

5. Bake for 2–2½ hours, stirring occasionally, or until the vegetables are tender and the cassoulet has thickened.

Turkey Chili

This protein-packed chili makes a great meal during exam period!

INGREDIENTS | SERVES 4

1 pound uncooked turkey breast
½ onion
2 cloves garlic
2 tablespoons chopped jalapeño peppers
1 (15- to 16-ounce can) white beans
1 (15- to 16-ounce can) chickpeas (also called garbanzo beans)
2 tablespoons olive oil
4 teaspoons ground cumin
1 teaspoon summer savory
1 teaspoon marjoram
½ pound ground turkey
4 cups gluten-free chicken broth
¼ cup white rice
Hot sauce, to taste
Salt and pepper, to taste
Grated Cheddar cheese, for garnish

1. Cut the turkey into ½" cubes. Mince the onion and garlic. Seed and chop the jalapeños. Drain and rinse the beans.

2. In a soup pot, heat the oil. Sauté the onion and garlic over medium heat for 3 minutes. Stir in the cumin, savory, and marjoram and cook for 30 seconds.

3. Add both kinds of turkey, sautéing until browned slightly.

4. Pour in the broth and stir in the rice and the jalapeños. Bring to a boil, reduce to a simmer, and cook for 30 minutes.

5. Add the beans, a dash of hot sauce, and salt and pepper to taste; simmer for another 10 minutes. Top with the grated cheese and serve.

Lemony Chicken

Delicately flavored Steamed Jasmine Rice (see Chapter 9) would make an excellent accompaniment to this dish. Prepare the rice while the chicken is simmering.

INGREDIENTS | SERVES 2

- 2 (7-ounce) boneless, skinless chicken breasts
- 4 tablespoons lemon juice, divided
- 2 teaspoons vegetable oil
- ½ small white onion, chopped
- 1 zucchini, sliced
- ½ cup gluten-free chicken broth
- 2 tablespoons tomato sauce
- ¼ teaspoon salt, or to taste
- ¼ teaspoon pepper, or to taste

Adjusting Recipes

When adjusting the portions of a recipe, remember that the quantity of food affects the total cooking time. For example, the cooking time for four potatoes will be longer than the cooking time for one.

1. Rinse the chicken breasts and pat dry. Place 2 tablespoons of the lemon juice in a resealable plastic bag. Add the chicken breasts. Seal the bag and refrigerate for 1 hour, turning the bag occasionally so that all the meat is covered. Remove the marinated chicken from the refrigerator and pat dry. Discard the marinade.

2. Heat the vegetable oil in a frying pan over medium heat. Add the onion and cook until tender. Add the chicken and cook until it turns white, about 5 minutes. Add the zucchini and cook for 1 minute.

3. Add the chicken broth, tomato sauce, remaining 2 tablespoons lemon juice, and salt and pepper. Cover and simmer for 20 minutes. Serve hot.

Simple Steak and Potatoes Dinner

You could also replace the baked potato with steamed broccoli or basic cooked long-grain rice.

INGREDIENTS | SERVES 4

8 ounces fresh brown mushrooms

1 clove garlic

4 (10-ounce) boneless rib-eye steaks

¼ cup gluten-free barbecue sauce (such as Sticky Fingers, KC Masterpiece, or Sweet Baby Ray's)

4 large baking potatoes

2 tablespoons olive oil

Easy Defrosting in the Microwave

If you plan to use the microwave for defrosting meat on a regular basis, be sure to wrap all your meat in plastic wrap that is marked as microwave safe. That way, it can go straight from freezer to microwave.

1. Preheat oven to broil. Wipe the mushrooms clean with a damp cloth and slice.

2. Peel the garlic and cut in half. Rub the steaks with the garlic. Place the steaks on a broiling pan and brush the tops with half of the barbecue sauce. Broil for 8–10 minutes on the top side, and then turn over and brush with the remaining barbecue sauce. Broil for 8–10 more minutes.

3. Begin preparing the potatoes and mushrooms after the steaks have finished cooking on the first side. Pierce the potatoes with a fork. Place on a microwave-safe plate or a paper towel and microwave on high for 10 minutes or until the potatoes are tender (the internal temperature should be 210°F).

4. Heat the olive oil in a frying pan over low-medium heat. Add the mushrooms and sauté over medium to medium-low heat until browned and tender. Serve all the food together.

Louisiana Seafood

This combination of seafood is reminiscent of a clam bake but is much easier to make.

INGREDIENTS | SERVES 4

2 shallots, chopped

3 cloves garlic, minced

¼ cup dry white wine

½ teaspoon dried basil

¼ teaspoon dried thyme

12 raw sea scallops

8 large raw shrimp

8 clams, scrubbed

8 mussels, debearded

2 (6-ounce) frozen lobster tails, thawed and chopped

2 tomatoes, chopped

3 cups hot cooked brown rice

1. In a large stock pot, combine the shallots, garlic, and wine, and bring to a simmer. Simmer until vegetables soften, about 5 minutes. Add the basil and thyme.

2. Add all the seafood except the lobster. Cover and cook for 6–8 minutes, shaking the pot frequently, until the shrimp curl, the scallops are opaque, and the clams and mussels open. Discard any clams and mussels that do not open.

3. Remove the cover and add the lobster and tomato. Cook and stir until the lobster is hot, about 2–3 minutes longer. Serve over hot cooked rice.

Why Louisiana?

The combination of rice and seafood is commonly found in Louisiana Creole cuisine, which is a melting pot that blends French, Spanish, Caribbean, Mediterranean, Indian, and African influences. For a taste of the real thing, take a trip to New Orleans for your next vacation!

Scallop and Pepper Stir-Fry

When making a stir-fry, make sure that you have all of the ingredients prepared before you start cooking since the cooking time is so short.

INGREDIENTS | SERVES 4

1 pound bay scallops
1 tablespoon cornstarch
¼ teaspoon salt
⅛ teaspoon cayenne pepper
1 tablespoon olive oil
1 red onion, chopped
2 cloves garlic, minced
1 green bell pepper, chopped
1 red bell pepper, chopped
2 cups cold cooked white rice
3 tablespoons apple juice
1 tablespoon lemon juice

1. In a medium bowl, combine the scallops with the cornstarch, salt, and cayenne pepper; toss to coat.

2. In a large frying pan or wok, heat olive oil over medium-high heat. Add the onion and garlic and stir-fry for 2 minutes.

3. Add the scallop mixture and the bell peppers and stir-fry until the scallops are just cooked, about 4–5 minutes.

4. Add the rice, and then sprinkle with apple juice and lemon juice. Stir-fry until the rice is heated through, about 2–4 minutes. Serve immediately.

Curried Shrimp and Vegetables

Adding lots of vegetables to seafood not only enhances the flavor,
but it increases the nutrition of a dish and lowers the fat content.

INGREDIENTS | SERVES 6

1 tablespoon olive oil
1 onion, chopped
3 cloves garlic, minced
1 tablespoon curry powder
½ teaspoon cinnamon
1½ cups water
2 carrots, sliced
2 Russet potatoes, peeled and cubed
1 zucchini, sliced
1 (14.5-ounce) can diced tomatoes
1 pound raw shrimp
4 cups hot cooked brown rice

1. In a large frying pan, heat oil over medium heat. Add onion and garlic; cook and stir until crisp-tender, about 4 minutes. Add curry powder and cinnamon; cook and stir for 1 minute longer.

2. Add water, carrots, and potatoes; bring to a simmer. Then reduce the heat to low, cover, and cook for 8–10 minutes or until carrots are crisp-tender. Add zucchini, tomatoes, and shrimp, cover again, and simmer for 5–8 minutes longer or until shrimp are pink.

3. Spoon rice onto individual plates and top with shrimp and vegetables; serve immediately.

Cooking with Curry

The flavors in curry powder are enhanced when they are heated, which is why the powder is often cooked in the first step of many Indian recipes. It's still good when uncooked, however. You can buy curry powder in many blends, from hot to mild. Curry powder is a blend of spices, and each blend is usually unique to a particular area of India.

Mexican Lasagna

Although this dish is relatively quick to prepare, you can also make the lasagna ahead of time and keep it covered in the refrigerator. This will require you to increase the baking time by 20–30 minutes. Many store-bought taco seasonings are not gluten-free, so make sure to read the label.

INGREDIENTS | SERVES 12

1¼ pounds lean ground beef
½ cup diced onion
½ cup diced red bell pepper
1½ cups frozen corn
1 (19-ounce) can kidney beans
2 tablespoons gluten-free taco seasoning
1½ cups salsa
1 cup sour cream
15 (4") gluten-free corn tortillas
3 cups shredded Cheddar cheese
Chopped cilantro, for garnish (optional)

Make Your Own Taco Seasoning

Mix together 2 tablespoons chili powder, 2 teaspoons ground cumin, 1 teaspoon each paprika and salt, and ½ teaspoon each garlic powder, onion powder, dried oregano, and ground black pepper. Store in an airtight container, and use in any recipes that call for taco seasoning.

1. Grease one 9" × 13" pan, and preheat the oven to 375°F.

2. In a large frying pan, cook the ground beef until nearly cooked. While it is still moist, add the onion, red pepper, and corn. Fry, stirring occasionally, until the onion is transparent and the corn is defrosted.

3. Add the kidney beans, taco seasoning, and salsa and continue stirring to heat throughout. Stir in the sour cream and set aside.

4. Cut 9 of the tortillas in half. This will allow you to have the tortilla layer going to the edge of your pan.

5. Line the bottom of your pan with 5 corn tortillas (6 halves and 2 whole), with the straight side of the halves facing the outside.

6. Top with half of the ground beef mixture.

7. Sprinkle on half of the cheese followed by another layer of corn tortillas.

8. Spread the remaining ground beef mixture over the lasagna.

9. Top with the third layer of corn tortillas and sprinkle with the remaining cheese.

10. Cover with foil and bake in preheated oven for 30 minutes. Allow to sit for 5 minutes before slicing and serving. Sprinkle with cilantro before serving if desired.

Sloppy Joes

Sloppy Joes are perfect for parties, as the meat can be kept warm in a slow cooker on low heat for hours. Just be sure to add more water if it seems to be getting too dry.

INGREDIENTS | SERVES 8

2 pounds lean ground beef

1½ teaspoons onion powder

½ teaspoon garlic powder

1 tablespoon gluten-free Worcestershire sauce

½ cup ketchup

1 teaspoon chili powder

¼ cup brown sugar

¾ cup water

2 tablespoons white vinegar

1 tablespoon yellow mustard

1 teaspoon salt

½ teaspoon ground black pepper

Gluten-free buns (such as Udi's, Rudi's, or Food For Life Gluten-Free English Muffins)

1. In a large frying pan, cook the ground beef over medium heat until completely browned. To eliminate a lot of the fat, you can spoon the beef into a colander and rinse under running hot water before returning it to the frying pan.

2. Add the rest of the ingredients. Bring to a boil, and then turn heat down to low and simmer for 20–30 minutes, stirring occasionally.

3. Serve on gluten-free buns with your favorite toppings.

Anti-Onion

By using dried garlic and onion powder, this recipe is full of great flavor and perfect for you if you don't like to see chopped onions in your food. If you wish, you can use ½ cup diced onion and 1 clove minced garlic in place of the dried powders.

Beef and Broccoli Stir-Fry

Ordering in Chinese food can be difficult when you are on a gluten-free diet.
But you can still make some of your favorite recipes at home, and it really doesn't take very long.

INGREDIENTS | SERVES 4

¼ cup water

¼ cup gluten-free soy sauce, such as La Choy

2 cloves garlic, minced

¼ teaspoon ground black pepper

1 pound stir-fry beef (or boneless round steak, cut into 3" strips)

2 tablespoons oil

½ cup chopped or thinly sliced onion

½ cup thinly sliced carrots

4 cups broccoli florets

1 cup cold water

¼ cup gluten-free soy sauce, such as La Choy

¼ cup brown sugar

1½ teaspoons ground ginger

1 teaspoon sesame oil

¼ teaspoon red pepper flakes (optional, adds some nice heat)

¼ cup cornstarch

1–2 teaspoons toasted sesame seeds

1. In a glass bowl, whisk together the ¼ cup water, ¼ cup soy sauce, garlic, and black pepper. Add the stir-fry beef strips and marinate for half an hour.

2. In a large frying pan or wok, heat the 2 tablespoons of oil over medium-high heat. Add the stir-fry beef and marinade, and fry until the meat is no longer pink, about 3–5 minutes.

3. Add the onion and carrots, and fry, while continuing to stir, for another 2 minutes. Add the broccoli and continue stirring and frying for an additional minute.

4. In a small bowl, whisk together the 1 cup cold water, the second ¼ cup soy sauce, brown sugar, ginger, sesame oil, red pepper flakes, and cornstarch. Pour this mixture over the beef and broccoli mixture, and cook until sauce thickens, about 2–3 more minutes.

5. Serve immediately over hot rice. Sprinkle with toasted sesame seeds before serving.

Chicken Stir-Fry

Use this simple, versatile recipe the next time you are craving Chinese takeout. Feel free to alter the vegetables to incorporate your favorites.

INGREDIENTS | SERVES 6

4 (4-ounce) boneless, skinless chicken breasts
2 tablespoons gluten-free soy sauce, such as La Choy
½ teaspoon ground ginger
¼ teaspoon garlic powder
3 tablespoons oil, divided
2 cups broccoli florets
1 cup bean sprouts
½ cup diced red bell pepper
1 cup thinly sliced carrots
1 small onion, chopped
1 clove garlic, minced
2 cups water
2 teaspoons gluten-free chicken bouillon granules
½ cup gluten-free soy sauce, such as La Choy
3 tablespoons cornstarch

1. Cut chicken into ½" strips and place in a resealable plastic bag. Combine 2 tablespoons gluten-free soy sauce, ground ginger, and garlic powder. Add to bag and shake well. Let marinate in refrigerator for at least 30 minutes.

2. In a large frying pan or wok, heat 1 tablespoon oil over medium-high heat. Add the chicken and marinade and stir-fry until the chicken is no longer pink, about 3–5 minutes. Remove from frying pan and keep warm.

3. Add the remaining 2 tablespoons oil and stir-fry the broccoli, bean sprouts, red pepper, carrots, onion, and garlic for 4–5 minutes or until crisp-tender. Return chicken to the wok.

4. In a large measuring cup, combine the water, chicken bouillon, ½ cup gluten-free soy sauce, and cornstarch. Pour into wok and continue stirring until the sauce thickens and is bubbly.

5. Serve over hot rice noodles or rice.

Cornmeal-Crusted Chicken

This is a wonderful, moist, and tender chicken that is great served with mashed potatoes or fries.

INGREDIENTS | SERVES 8

1 (3-pound) chicken, with skin on, cut up
2 cups buttermilk
½ cup gluten-free cornmeal (such as Bob's Red Mill)
¼ cup brown rice flour
3 tablespoons cornstarch
1 teaspoon salt
1 teaspoon ground black pepper
1 teaspoon onion powder
½ teaspoon garlic powder

Make This Dairy-Free

You can make vegan buttermilk by adding 1 tablespoon lemon juice to 2 cups of almond or rice milk; let stand for 10 minutes, stir, and use. Don't be alarmed if the lemon juice causes the milk to separate; just stir it back together.

1. Place chicken in a large glass baking dish and pour buttermilk over the chicken. Cover and refrigerate at least 8 hours.

2. When ready to bake, preheat oven to 375°F. Line a large baking sheet with heavy-duty foil and spray the foil with nonstick cooking spray; set aside.

3. In a shallow bowl, combine all remaining ingredients and mix well. Remove chicken from buttermilk, shake off excess, and discard buttermilk. Dredge chicken in the cornmeal mixture to coat.

4. Place chicken, skin-side up, on prepared baking sheet. Bake 45–55 minutes or until chicken is thoroughly cooked and coating is a deep golden brown. Let stand 5 minutes before serving.

Homemade Bean and Vegetable Burgers

Homemade bean burgers are much better than their frozen store-bought counterpart, and you know these don't contain any extra fillers.

INGREDIENTS | SERVES 4

1 (15-ounce) can dark red kidney beans, drained

1 large Yukon Gold potato, cooked and cooled

⅓ cup gluten-free cornmeal (such as Bob's Red Mill)

⅓ cup fresh or defrosted frozen peas

2 tablespoons minced onion

¼ teaspoon ground chipotle

¼ teaspoon paprika

¼ teaspoon freshly ground black pepper

¼ teaspoon sea salt

2 tablespoons apple cider vinegar

2 tablespoons oil

1. In a medium bowl, mash the beans and potato together using a potato masher. Add the remaining ingredients. Mix and form into four patties.

2. Heat the oil in a frying pan. Cook the burgers, flipping once, until cooked through and browned on both sides (about 5–7 minutes per side).

Chicken and Bean Tacos

Read the package on the taco shells to be sure they are gluten-free.
Let your friends assemble their own tacos so they can pick their own toppings.

INGREDIENTS | SERVES 8

2 boneless, skinless chicken breasts

½ teaspoon salt

⅛ teaspoon ground black pepper

1 tablespoon cornstarch

2 tablespoons olive oil

1 tablespoon lemon juice

½ cup chopped onion

½ yellow bell pepper, chopped

1 (15-ounce) can black beans, drained and rinsed

1 cup salsa

8 gluten-free corn taco shells

2 cups shredded lettuce

1 cup chopped tomatoes

½ cup sour cream

1 cup shredded Cheddar cheese

1. Preheat oven to 350°F. Cut chicken into 1" cubes and sprinkle with salt, pepper, and cornstarch. Heat olive oil in large frying pan and add chicken and lemon juice. Cook and stir until almost cooked, about 4 minutes; remove from frying pan.

2. Add onion and bell pepper to frying pan; cook and stir 4–5 minutes or until crisp-tender. Return chicken to frying pan along with beans and salsa; bring to a simmer. Simmer until chicken is cooked, about 3–5 minutes longer.

3. Meanwhile, heat taco shells as directed on the package. When shells are hot, make tacos with chicken mixture, lettuce, tomatoes, sour cream, and cheese. Serve immediately.

Pecan-Crusted Chicken

*This pecan crust recipe is quite versatile. It works for fish as well as chicken,
and other nuts can be substituted for different flavors.*

INGREDIENTS | SERVES 4

1 cup finely chopped pecans
2 large eggs, beaten
4 boneless, skinless chicken breasts

1. Preheat the oven to 350°F.

2. Place the chopped nuts in a shallow bowl and the eggs in a separate shallow bowl.

3. Dip each chicken breast in egg and then in nuts. Place coated chicken breasts in a shallow baking dish.

4. Bake for 25 minutes and serve.

Spicy Chicken Burgers

*You can substitute ground turkey or pork for the chicken.
Adjust the quantity of pepper flakes to control the spiciness.*

INGREDIENTS | SERVES 4

1 pound ground chicken breast
¼ cup finely chopped yellow onion
¼ cup finely chopped red bell pepper
1 teaspoon minced garlic
¼ cup thinly sliced scallions
½ teaspoon red pepper flakes
Freshly ground black pepper, to taste

1. Clean and oil the broiler rack. Preheat the broiler to medium.

2. Combine all the ingredients in a medium-size bowl, mixing lightly. Form the mixture into four patties.

3. Broil the burgers for 4–5 minutes per side until firm through the center and the juices run clear. Transfer to a plate and tent with tinfoil to keep warm. Allow to rest for 1–2 minutes before serving.

Ginger-Orange Chicken Breast

This recipe is great chilled, sliced, and served on a crispy green salad.

INGREDIENTS | SERVES 4

4 (5-ounce) skinless, boneless chicken breasts
2 tablespoons olive oil
½ teaspoon seasoned salt
Freshly ground black pepper, to taste
2 cloves garlic, minced
2 tablespoons grated ginger
2 teaspoons orange zest
½ cup 100-percent orange juice

Working with Chicken

Fresh boneless, skinless breasts are available in the meat section of your grocer. Use a good, reputable brand and check the freshness date. Prior to cooking or preparing, always rinse the meat under cold running water and pat dry with paper towels.

1. Rinse the chicken under cold running water and pat dry with paper towels.

2. Heat the olive oil in a small nonstick frying pan over medium-high heat. Season the chicken with salt and pepper and add to the pan. Brown the chicken, turning it once, about 8 minutes per side. Transfer the chicken to a plate and keep warm.

3. Add the garlic to the pan and cook for about 1 minute, stirring frequently to prevent burning. Add the ginger, zest, and juice, and bring to a simmer.

4. Add the chicken and any reserved juices and heat through, about 4–5 minutes. Cut through the bottom of the chicken to make sure it is cooked. Adjust seasoning to taste. Serve hot with the sauce.

CHAPTER 8

Vegetarian and Vegan Options

Stuffed Eggplant with Ricotta and Spices

This dish is also known as Eggplant Sicilian. It freezes beautifully and is very delicious. If you prefer more of a crispy crust on your eggplant, try using gluten-free cornmeal instead of brown rice flour for dredging.

INGREDIENTS | SERVES 4

2 medium eggplants, peeled, cut in 16 round slices (8 each), and salted

1 cup brown rice flour

Freshly ground black pepper, to taste

¼ cup olive oil, or as needed

2 cups tomato sauce

1 pound ricotta cheese

1 cup grated Parmesan cheese, divided

2 eggs

1 tablespoon dried oregano

1 cup shredded mozzarella cheese

Smaller Is Sweeter

The smaller eggplants now available are much sweeter and not old enough to have grown bitter. Also, many have few seeds. They come in pale cream, lavender, and purple, all the way from egg-size to long and skinny. All are good!

1. Stack the salted eggplant slices on a plate and put another plate with a weight on top to press the brown liquid out of them.

2. Mix the flour and pepper, then dredge the eggplant slices in the flour mixture. Fry the slices in the olive oil, removing to paper towels as they are browned.

3. Preheat the oven to 325°F. Prepare a 2-quart casserole dish or a 10" × 10" glass pan with nonstick spray and cover bottom with a thin layer of tomato sauce.

4. In a large bowl, mix the ricotta cheese, ½ cup of the Parmesan, eggs, and oregano. Place 1 tablespoon of the egg-cheese mixture on each slice of eggplant and roll, placing seam-side down in the baking dish.

5. Spread with sauce, sprinkle with the rest of the Parmesan and the mozzarella, and bake for 35 minutes.

Stuffed Artichokes with Lemon and Olives

Artichokes have a way of making everything around them taste delicious.
They can be eaten with just a little butter, mayonnaise, or lemon juice.
You can make this a vegan meal by omitting the egg and using vegan margarine instead of butter.

INGREDIENTS | **SERVES 4 AS AN ENTRÉE,
OR 8 AS AN APPETIZER**

4 large artichokes, trimmed and split lengthwise

4 quarts water

½ lemon

1 cup cooked rice

10 green olives, chopped

10 kalamata olives, chopped

2 tablespoons minced parsley

3 tablespoons butter or vegan margarine, melted

1 teaspoon garlic salt

Pepper, to taste

1 egg (optional)

1. Fill a pot with the water and squeeze the lemon into it, tossing in the rind afterward. Boil the artichokes in the lemon-water for 20 minutes. Drain and lay on a baking sheet, cut-side up.

2. Preheat the oven to 350°F.

3. Mix the rest of the ingredients (including the egg, if using) together in a large bowl.

4. Spoon the filling over the artichokes, pressing between the leaves. Bake for 15 minutes or until hot.

Grilled Portobello Mushrooms

These big, meaty mushrooms are great sliced over salad, stuffed, or chopped into sauce.

INGREDIENTS | **SERVES 4**

4 large (4"–5" in diameter) portobello mushrooms, wiped clean, stems removed

1 cup balsamic vinaigrette

Salt and pepper, to taste

Mushrooms and Protein

Mushrooms are not really high in protein, but they are filling. The large portobello mushrooms are great for grilling or stuffing with all kinds of goodies. They make excellent bases for rice, quinoa, eggs, and vegetables.

1. Marinate the mushrooms in the vinaigrette and salt and pepper for 1–2 hours, covered, in the refrigerator.

2. Preheat your grill to glowing coals, or set your gas grill to low.

3. Grill mushrooms stem-side down for about 8 minutes. Turn and grill for 6–8 minutes more. Slice and serve.

Indian Vegetable Cakes

This is a great way to eat your vegetables! A nonstick pan helps to prevent sticking. Sour cream makes a very good garnish.

INGREDIENTS | SERVES 4–6

1 tablespoon olive oil

1 (10-ounce) package frozen chopped spinach, thawed, moisture squeezed out

½ box (5 ounces) frozen baby peas, thawed

½ bunch scallions, chopped

1 teaspoon curry powder

Salt and hot pepper sauce, to taste

¼ cup gluten-free cornmeal (such as Bob's Red Mill)

5 extra-large eggs, well beaten

½ cup Parmesan cheese

1. Heat olive oil in a nonstick pan over medium heat.

2. In a large bowl, mix together all remaining ingredients except the Parmesan cheese. Form into patties.

3. Drop the patties, three or four at a time, into the pan and fry until delicately browned. Turn and sprinkle with cheese.

Corn and Spinach Pockets Stuffed
with Cheese and Artichokes

This is a creative and exciting vegetarian and gluten-free dish you can make in no time!

INGREDIENTS | SERVES 8

1 (10-ounce) box frozen artichoke hearts

1 (10-ounce) box frozen spinach, thawed, moisture squeezed out

1 cup ricotta cheese

4 ounces cream cheese

¼ cup minced chives

¼ teaspoon freshly ground nutmeg

Salt and pepper, to taste

1 egg

8 large (8"–9" in diameter) Brown Rice Crepes (see Chapter 2)

1 egg, beaten, for sealing pockets

Selecting and Preparing Artichokes

Look for artichokes that are tightly closed. Take a pair of kitchen scissors and clip off the sharp points. You can use a knife to cut off the tops. Artichokes are hearty when stuffed with many kinds of delicious foods. If you eat fish, salmon mixed with rice makes an excellent stuffing.

1. Cook the artichoke hearts according to package directions until soft. Place in a food processor with the spinach and blend together, slowly adding the cheeses, chives, seasonings, and egg.

2. Preheat the oven to 350°F. Lay out the crepes on a nonstick baking sheet or one covered with a sheet of aluminum foil.

3. Divide the filling among the crepes, spooning onto one half and leaving the other half plain. Be sure to leave a little space at the edges for sealing.

4. Wet the edges of the crepes with beaten egg. Fold over and press lightly to seal, and then bake for 20 minutes or until well browned and filling is bubbling out.

Spinach with Baked Eggs and Cheese

This is an excellent brunch, lunch, or supper. Everyone loves it,
and even after a tough day of classes and studying, it's easy to put together.

INGREDIENTS | SERVES 4

1½ cups gluten-free cornbread crumbs

3 (10-ounce) packages frozen spinach, thawed, moisture squeezed out

2 tablespoons butter or margarine, melted

½ cup shredded Swiss cheese

½ teaspoon nutmeg

Salt and pepper, to taste

1 cup heavy cream

8 eggs

1. Preheat the oven to 325°F. Prepare a 10" × 10" glass baking dish or gratin pan with nonstick spray. Sprinkle it with cornbread crumbs.

2. In a large bowl, mix the spinach, butter or margarine, cheese, nutmeg, and salt and pepper together. Stir in the heavy cream. Spread the spinach-cheese mixture in the bottom of the prepared pan.

3. Using the back of a tablespoon, make 8 depressions in the spinach mixture. Crack the eggs into the depressions. Bake for 20 minutes or until the eggs are firm but not hard.

Potato Frittata with Cheese and Herbs

Use both nonstick spray and butter in this recipe, or the starch in the potatoes will stick. You can experiment with different herbs and cheeses.

INGREDIENTS | SERVES 4

1 large Yukon Gold potato, peeled
4 teaspoons butter
Salt and pepper, to taste
6 eggs
½ cup grated Parmesan cheese
6 sage leaves, minced
Fresh herbs, extra cheese, and sour cream, for garnish

Striking Yukon Gold

Yukon Gold potatoes were developed in the 1970s at the University of Guelph in Ontario, Canada. They were initially slow to capture the market but now are widely popular, particularly suited for baking, salad, and soup.

1. Using a mandolin or sharp knife, slice the potato as thinly as possible. Prepare a heavy 12" ovenproof frying pan, first with nonstick spray, then with butter.

2. Add the potatoes, making a thin layer, and season with salt and pepper. Cook over medium heat for 10 minutes—this will be the crust.

3. Beat the eggs well; add the cheese and sage. Pour egg mixture over the potatoes and turn down heat to the lowest possible setting. Cook for 10 minutes.

4. When the eggs have set, run the frittata under the broiler until golden brown on top. Cut into wedges and serve at once with garnishes.

Frittata with Asparagus and Two Cheeses

Some matches are made in heaven, and asparagus with eggs and cheese is a divine combination.

INGREDIENTS | SERVES 4

1 (10-ounce) box frozen chopped asparagus or 10 ounces fresh asparagus

2 tablespoons butter

6 eggs

1 cup grated Cheddar cheese

¼ cup shredded Monterey jack or pepper jack cheese

1 teaspoon minced lemon rind

Salt and pepper, to taste

Use Up Your Leftovers

The frittata is a staple in Italy—putting a lot of eggs together with leftover or fresh vegetables is a fine way of using every precious bit of food. A frittata can be jazzed up with herbs, cheeses, and hot red pepper flakes. The only thing to remember about frittatas is that just about anything goes!

1. Cook the asparagus according to package directions. If you are using fresh asparagus, trim off all of the woody ends and boil for 10 minutes. Drain and chop.

2. Prepare a heavy 12" ovenproof frying pan with nonstick spray and then melt the butter over medium-high heat.

3. In a medium bowl, beat the eggs. Mix in the cheeses, lemon rind, and salt and pepper.

4. Pour the egg-cheese mixture into the pan, distribute asparagus, and reduce heat, cooking very slowly for 10–15 minutes.

5. Run under preheated broiler for 10 seconds or until nicely browned.

Polenta with Chilies and Cheddar Cheese

This has a spicy Southwestern flavor. You'll love it with ham, pork, or barbecue.
It's also good with split-pea soup.

INGREDIENTS | SERVES 6–7

1 recipe Classic Polenta with Herbs and Parmesan (see this chapter), prepared to be firm

1 cup mild, medium, or hot salsa

4 jalapeño peppers, cored, seeded, and chopped

1½ cups coarsely grated sharp Cheddar cheese

Sour cream, for garnish (1 tablespoon per square of polenta)

1. When the polenta is firm, cut in portion-size squares and place on an oiled cookie sheet.

2. Preheat the oven to 350°F.

3. In a large bowl, mix together the salsa, peppers, and cheese. Spoon over the top of the squares of polenta.

4. Bake until very hot and the cheese is melted in the sauce. Arrange on plates and spoon a dollop of sour cream over each.

Snow Peas with Water Chestnuts and Ginger

This tasty side dish is very fast and good. It's a boon to the busy student who wants fresh vegetables but has little time.

INGREDIENTS | SERVES 4

1 pound snow pea pods, ends trimmed

½ cup peanut oil

1 (8-ounce) can water chestnuts, drained, rinsed, and sliced

½ cup unsalted peanuts

2 tablespoons gluten-free soy sauce (such as La Choy)

1 teaspoon lemon juice

1 tablespoon minced fresh gingerroot

Tabasco or other red pepper sauce, to taste

1. Place the snow pea pods in a hot wok or frying pan with the oil. Stir to coat, then add the water chestnuts and peanuts, stirring again.

2. Continue cooking, and after 5 minutes, add the rest of the ingredients. Mix well and serve hot or at room temperature.

Cheese and Milk in Asian Cooking

The reason that cheese and milk are practically nonexistent in Asian cooking is that Asian countries do not have many dairy cows. In some areas, water buffalo work hard and produce milk, too. Water buffalo in Italy provide the milk for a wonderful mozzarella cheese. Asians substitute tofu for meat, and what meat they do eat is stretched with vegetables and rice. Fish is popular in lake and seaside communities. Americans have adapted Asian flavors in a popular fusion food.

Chinese Cabbage with Sesame

Chinese cabbage, also called Napa cabbage, is wonderful cooked or served raw in salads. It's pale green, mild, leafy, and very good for you!

INGREDIENTS | SERVES 4

2 tablespoons sesame seed oil

2 tablespoons canola or other light oil

1 tablespoon sesame seeds

1–1½-pound head Chinese (Napa) cabbage, washed and thinly sliced

Juice of ½ lemon

2 cloves garlic, minced

Salt and pepper, to taste

Gluten-free soy sauce (such as La Choy), to taste

1. Place the oils in a hot wok or frying pan. Add the sesame seeds and toast for 2 minutes.

2. Stir in the cabbage, lemon juice, and garlic. Toss until cabbage is just wilted, about 4 minutes. Add the salt and pepper and soy sauce and serve.

Polenta with Sun-Dried Tomatoes and Basil

The fascinating thing about polenta is that you can change the seasonings and/or toppings and fry, grill, or broil and have a different dish, based on polenta, time after time.

INGREDIENTS | MAKES 12 SQUARES

8 ounces sun-dried tomatoes in oil, finely chopped

20 basil leaves, rinsed

2 cloves garlic

Extra olive oil, if necessary

1 recipe Classic Polenta with Herbs and Parmesan (see this chapter), prepared to be firm

1 cup grated mozzarella cheese

1. Preheat oven to 350°F.

2. Whirl the tomatoes, basil, and garlic in a food processor. This should be chunky, not puréed. Add extra olive oil if too dry to process. Spread the tomato mixture over the polenta and cut into squares.

3. Place the squares on a cookie sheet that you have buttered or sprayed with nonstick spray. Bake for 20 minutes.

4. At the last minute, sprinkle the mozzarella over the top and bake until melted. Serve immediately.

Classic Polenta with Herbs and Parmesan

Use 7 cups of water if you want soft polenta the consistency of mashed potatoes; use 6½ cups if you prefer it firm enough to cut into squares to fry, broil, or grill.

INGREDIENTS | SERVES 4–6

6½ or 7 cups water

2 tablespoons salt

2 cups yellow gluten-free cornmeal (such as Bob's Red Mill)

2–4 ounces unsalted butter

2 tablespoons dried herbs or 1 tablespoon each chopped fresh basil, rosemary, and parsley

½ cup freshly grated Parmesan cheese

Freshly ground black pepper, to taste

The Staple of Lombardy

Polenta has been the staple food of Lombardy, at the foot of the Italian Alps, for three centuries. Thanks to Columbus and his sailors, corn, peppers, and other now-common staples have amplified the diet of much of Europe.

1. Bring the water to a boil.

2. Add salt, and using your hand to drop the cornmeal into the boiling water, let the cornmeal slip slowly between your fingers to make a very slim stream. You should be able to see each grain. Don't dump the cornmeal into the water or you will get a glue-like mass.

3. Stir constantly while adding the cornmeal. Reduce heat to low for a simmer and keep stirring for about 20 minutes as it thickens.

4. Stir in the butter, herbs, Parmesan cheese, and pepper. If you're making soft polenta, serve immediately. If you're making firm polenta, spread in a 9" × 13" lasagna pan that has been prepared with nonstick spray. Chill for 3 hours or overnight. Cut into sections and either fry, broil, or grill.

Easy Eggplant Parmigiana

This quick and easy version of the Italian classic is made with nondairy cheese shreds for vegetarians who don't eat dairy products. Unfortunately, melted nondairy cheese can have a slightly rubbery texture, so vegetarians who do consume dairy may want to stick with regular mozzarella.

INGREDIENTS | SERVES 2–4

1 medium eggplant

½ teaspoon dried basil

½ teaspoon dried oregano

⅛ teaspoon garlic salt, or to taste

1 cup spaghetti sauce

1 cup grated mozzarella or nondairy substitute such as Daiya (which does not contain soy)

¼ cup nondairy Parmesan cheese substitute or blanched almond flour (such as Honeyville)

1. Preheat oven to 350°F. Spray an 8" × 8" baking pan with nonstick cooking spray.

2. Wash the eggplant and cut into slices about ¼" thick. Stir the dried basil, dried oregano, and garlic salt into the spaghetti sauce.

3. Lay half the eggplant slices in the prepared baking pan. Spoon half the spaghetti sauce over the top. Repeat layers with remaining eggplant and sauce.

4. Cover the eggplant with foil and bake for 20 minutes or until tender. Remove from the oven. Uncover and sprinkle the soy mozzarella on top.

5. Bake for another 3–5 minutes, until the cheese melts. Sprinkle with the Parmesan cheese substitute or blanched almond flour and serve.

Indian Curried Lentil Soup

This lentil soup is perfect as is or perhaps paired with rice or some warmed Indian flatbread.

INGREDIENTS | SERVES 4

1 onion, diced

1 carrot, sliced

3 whole cloves

2 tablespoons vegan margarine or coconut oil

1 teaspoon cumin

1 teaspoon turmeric

1 cup yellow or green lentils

2¾ cups gluten-free vegetable broth

2 large tomatoes, chopped

1 teaspoon salt

¼ teaspoon black pepper

1 teaspoon lemon juice

1. In a large soup or stock pot, sauté the onion, carrot, and cloves in margarine or coconut oil until onions are just turning soft, about 3 minutes. Add cumin and turmeric and toast for 1 minute, stirring constantly to avoid burning.

2. Reduce heat to medium-low and add lentils, vegetable broth, tomatoes, and salt. Bring to a simmer, cover, and cook for 35–40 minutes, until lentils are done.

3. Season with black pepper and lemon juice just before serving.

Cream of Carrot Soup with Coconut

This carrot soup will have you begging for more. The addition of coconut milk transforms an ordinary carrot and ginger soup into an unexpected treat.

INGREDIENTS | SERVES 6

3 medium carrots, chopped

1 sweet potato, chopped

1 yellow onion, chopped

3½ cups gluten-free vegetable broth

3 cloves garlic, minced

2 teaspoons minced fresh ginger

1 (14-ounce) can coconut milk

1 teaspoon salt

¾ teaspoon cinnamon (optional)

Eat Carrots for Your Eyes

In addition to being crunchy and tasty, carrots are also really good for you. They're rich in dietary fiber, antioxidants, and minerals, as well as vitamin A, which helps maintain your vision for all that reading you'll be doing. An urban legend says that eating large amounts of carrots will allow you to see in the dark! While this isn't exactly true, it is a good indicator that you should work more carrots into your diet.

1. In a large soup or stock pot, bring the carrots, sweet potato, and onion to a simmer in the vegetable broth. Add garlic and ginger, cover, and heat for 20–25 minutes, until carrots and potatoes are soft.

2. Allow to cool slightly, then transfer to a blender and purée until smooth.

3. Return soup to pot. Over very low heat, stir in the coconut milk and salt, stirring well to combine. Heat just until heated through, another 3–4 minutes.

4. Garnish with cinnamon just before serving if desired.

Spicy Southwestern Two-Bean Salad

This cold bean salad with Tex-Mex flavors is even better the next day—if it lasts that long!

INGREDIENTS | SERVES 6–8

1 (15-ounce) can black beans, drained and rinsed

1 (15-ounce) can kidney beans, drained and rinsed

1 red or yellow bell pepper, chopped

1 large tomato, diced

⅔ cup corn (fresh, canned, or frozen)

⅓ cup olive oil

¼ cup lime juice

½ teaspoon chili powder

½ teaspoon garlic powder

¼ teaspoon cayenne pepper

½ teaspoon salt

¼ cup chopped fresh cilantro

1 avocado, diced

1. In a large bowl, combine the black beans, kidney beans, bell pepper, tomato, and corn.

2. In a separate small bowl, whisk together the olive oil, lime juice, chili powder, garlic powder, cayenne, and salt.

3. Pour olive oil mixture over bean mixture, tossing to coat. Stir in fresh cilantro.

4. Chill for at least 1 hour before serving, to allow flavors to mingle.

5. Add avocado and gently toss again just before serving.

Make It a Pasta Salad

Guess what? This recipe can also double as another kind of salad. Just omit the avocado and add some cooked gluten-free pasta and extra dressing to turn it into a high-protein Tex-Mex pasta salad! Have this salad for lunch or a light dinner, and take the rest for leftovers the next day.

Veggie-Stuffed Peppers

*When you place the peppers on the baking pan,
add a little water to the pan so that the peppers don't burn.*

INGREDIENTS | SERVES 4

4 green bell peppers

6 cups water

1 (15-ounce) can pinto beans, rinsed and drained

2 cups whole kernel corn

¾ cup low-fat shredded Cheddar cheese or nondairy Cheddar cheese substitute (such as Daiya)

½ tablespoon vegetable oil

1 clove garlic, crushed

½ onion, chopped

1 teaspoon black pepper

1. Preheat the oven to 375°F.

2. Cut off the tops of the green peppers. Remove the seeds.

3. Boil the water; add peppers and cook for 5 minutes. Remove peppers and place upside down on a paper towel to drain.

4. Mix all remaining ingredients in a medium bowl. Divide mixture evenly among peppers and stuff them. Place peppers on a baking dish, filled-side up, and bake about 20 minutes. Serve hot.

No Meat?

Stuffed peppers is another meal that is traditionally made with meat but doesn't have to be. In fact, there are lots of varieties, many including rice. If you're vegetarian or simply looking for a lighter meal, try this meatless version. You'll find it's just as satisfying as any other variation.

Basic Polenta with Butter and Cheese

*You can enjoy this basic polenta by itself, with different kinds of cheese,
or with added meat or veggies. To make this recipe dairy-free, use blanched almond flour
instead of cheese. To make this recipe vegan, use vegan margarine instead of butter.*

INGREDIENTS | SERVES 4

3½ cups water

1 teaspoon salt

1 cup coarsely ground yellow gluten-free cornmeal (such as Bob's Red Mill)

1 tablespoon butter or olive oil

2 tablespoons Parmesan or fontina cheese, grated

Pepper, to taste

Parsley, for garnish

1. Bring the water to a boil. Add salt. Stir in the cornmeal in a thin stream, stirring constantly. Reduce heat to low; continue to stir for 20 minutes or until the polenta comes away from the pot.

2. Stir in the butter or olive oil, cheese, pepper, and parsley.

What Is Polenta?

In some parts of Italy, polenta is used more than pasta! It is simply cornmeal cooked in boiling water until soft and fluffy like mashed potatoes. When polenta is cooled, it stiffens up, making it useful for frying or grilling. This classic can be used instead of pasta or potatoes. Serve as a base for stews, veggies, or pasta sauces.

Polenta with Broccoli Rabe

*Broccoli rabe is a leafy vegetable whose florets resemble those of broccoli.
It packs a wonderful and slightly bitter, acidic punch that contrasts with the mildness of the polenta.*

INGREDIENTS | SERVES 4

1 pound broccoli rabe

1 quart boiling, salted water

2 tablespoons olive oil

2 cloves garlic, minced

Juice of ½ lemon

Red pepper flakes, to taste

Basic Polenta with Butter and Cheese (see this chapter)

1. Rinse the broccoli rabe and cut into 1½" pieces, trimming off very bottoms of stems. Drop the broccoli rabe into the boiling water and cook for 5 minutes. Shock in cold water. Drain thoroughly.

2. Heat the olive oil and sauté garlic over medium heat. Add the lemon juice, pepper flakes, and drained broccoli rabe. Cook and stir until well coated.

3. Serve over hot polenta.

Twice-Baked Greek Potatoes

*Potatoes always make a great side dish, but when you can give them some flair,
they really stand out at the meal. These Twice-Baked Greek Potatoes take on the traditional
flavors of Greece, by using spices like oregano, thyme, and basil, topped with feta cheese.*

INGREDIENTS | SERVES 4

4 large Russet potatoes, baked

1 cup crumbled feta cheese

1 cup sour cream (or plain yogurt)

½ teaspoon ground black pepper

1 teaspoon dried oregano

1 teaspoon dried thyme

½ teaspoon dried basil

2 cloves garlic, minced (or ¾ teaspoon garlic powder)

1 medium tomato, chopped

¼ cup chopped black olives (optional)

¼ cup chopped green onion

How to Bake Potatoes

You can wrap washed and dried potatoes in foil and bake in a 400°F oven until a knife can easily be poked into the potato, about 1 hour. Or, you can bake them in the slow cooker with 2 tablespoons of water on low heat for 8–10 hours. Both methods will give you potatoes that are tender when a knife is inserted, and they are then ready to spoon out and season.

1. Let hot, baked potatoes sit for about 15 minutes before handling. Carefully cut about 1" off the top of the potatoes lengthwise. Scoop the potato out of the skin into a large mixing bowl, leaving the skins intact. Place the scooped-out potato skins in a single layer on a baking dish.

2. Add the feta cheese, sour cream, pepper, herbs, and garlic to the potatoes, and mash using a potato masher until smooth. Stir in the tomato, olives, and green onion. Spoon filling back into potato shells until they are nicely rounded on the tops.

3. Place potatoes in preheated 400°F oven and bake for 15–20 minutes or until heated throughout. Serve immediately.

Pesto Potatoes

This flavorful side dish is delicious, warm, and creamy. Pair it with your favorite meal.

INGREDIENTS | SERVES 8

4 pounds Russet potatoes
2 tablespoons olive oil
1 small yellow onion, chopped
3 cloves garlic, minced
½ cup basil pesto
¼ cup plain yogurt

Make Your Own Basil Pesto

In a food processor, grind together 1½ cups packed fresh basil leaves, 1 cup packed baby spinach leaves, 3 cloves garlic, 2 tablespoons lemon juice, ½ teaspoon salt, and ⅛ teaspoon pepper. With motor running, add ½–¾ cup olive oil until desired consistency is reached. By hand, stir in ¼ cup Parmesan cheese and 2 tablespoons water, if needed. Store tightly covered in refrigerator for up to three days. Freeze for longer storage.

1. Preheat the oven to 400°F. Scrub potatoes and cut into 1" pieces.

2. In a large roasting pan, combine the potatoes with the olive oil, onion, and garlic. Roast for 30 minutes, and then turn with a spatula. Roast 30–40 minutes longer or until potatoes are tender and turning brown on the edges.

3. In a serving bowl, combine pesto and yogurt and mix well. Add the hot potato mixture and toss to coat. Serve immediately.

Smashed Potatoes

These rustic potatoes aren't mashed perfectly smooth.
The skins are left on, which adds nutrients and fiber.

INGREDIENTS | SERVES 6

6 Yukon Gold potatoes

3 tablespoons olive oil

3 cloves garlic, minced

2 shallots, minced

1 (3-ounce) package cream cheese, softened

2–4 tablespoons milk

½ teaspoon salt

⅛ teaspoon black pepper

1. Scrub potatoes and cut into 1" pieces. Bring a large pot of water to a boil. Add potatoes; bring back to a simmer. Simmer 10–20 minutes or until potatoes are tender when pierced with a fork. Drain, and then return potatoes to the hot pot.

2. Meanwhile, in a small saucepan, heat olive oil over medium heat; sauté garlic and shallots for 2–3 minutes. Place pot with hot potatoes over medium heat and, using a fork or potato masher, mash in the garlic mixture. Leave some pieces of the potatoes whole.

3. Stir in the cream cheese, 2 tablespoons milk, salt, and pepper; add more milk if necessary for desired consistency. Serve immediately, or you can keep these potatoes warm in a double boiler over simmering water for about an hour.

Chipotle-Lime Mashed Sweet Potato

If you don't like sweet potatoes, you can easily substitute other vegetables such as rutabagas, turnips, or beets. Additionally, cauliflower makes a great fake "mashed potato" substitute.

INGREDIENTS | SERVES 10

3 pounds sweet potatoes
1½ tablespoons coconut oil
1¼ teaspoons chipotle powder
Juice from ½ large lime

1. Peel the sweet potatoes and cut into cubes.

2. Steam the cubes until soft, approximately 5–8 minutes. Transfer to a large bowl.

3. In a small saucepan, heat coconut oil and whisk in the chipotle powder and lime juice.

4. Pour the mixture into the bowl with the sweet potato cubes and mash with fork or potato masher.

Citrus-Steamed Carrots

Figs are the fruit of gods and goddesses. Enjoy the pleasure yourself after a long night of studying!

INGREDIENTS | SERVES 6

1 pound carrots
1 cup orange juice
2 tablespoons lemon juice
2 tablespoons lime juice
3 fresh figs
1 tablespoon extra-virgin olive oil
1 tablespoon capers

1. Peel and julienne the carrots. In a pot, combine the citrus juices over medium-high heat. Add the carrots, cover, and steam until al dente. Remove from heat and let cool.

2. Cut the figs into wedges. Mound the carrots on serving plates and arrange the figs around the carrots. Sprinkle the olive oil and capers on top, and serve.

Roasted Asparagus

Use thicker asparagus to withstand the heat of the grill.
Be sure to remove the woody ends of the stalks first.

INGREDIENTS | SERVES 6

2 bunches asparagus, trimmed
1 tablespoon extra-virgin olive oil
1 teaspoon salt
Freshly ground black pepper, to taste
Lemon juice, to taste (optional)

1. Preheat the oven to 425°F.

2. In a 9" × 13" baking pan, toss the asparagus with the oil and season with salt and pepper. Bake for 15–20 minutes. Remove from oven and toss with lemon juice if desired. Serve immediately.

Asparagus

Asparagus is low in calories and sodium, and offers numerous vitamins and minerals, most notably folate and potassium. The stalks also offer a blast of inflammation-fighting antioxidants.

CHAPTER 9

Pasta and Grains

Vegetable Lasagna Primavera with Pasta Substitute

*This recipe takes very little time and is excellent for
a big dinner with friends. It's also great for vegetarians.*

INGREDIENTS | SERVES 6–8

4 eggs, divided

½ teaspoon table salt or sea salt, or to taste

¼ teaspoon pepper, or to taste

1½ cups milk or water

1 cup brown rice flour

Butter or oil, for greasing the griddle

1 pound ricotta cheese

½ cup Parmesan cheese

2 cups chopped raw mixed fresh vegetables (such as scallions, zucchini, fresh spinach, and young peas)

½ cup finely chopped fresh parsley

1½ cups Basic Cream Sauce (see sidebar for Mushroom, Ham, and Cheese Crepes in Chapter 2)

1 cup shredded mozzarella cheese

A Versatile Pasta

Any sauce that you would use on wheat pasta can be used on a gluten-free rice pasta—from a rich Alfredo sauce to a robust marinara sauce.

1. Mix 2 of the eggs, salt, pepper, milk or water, and brown rice flour in a blender and process until smooth.

2. Using a well-greased griddle, pour out the batter, fry until firm, and cut into 10" strips that are 2" wide. Turn using an extra-large, long spatula. As you finish, place the strips on a baking dish that has been prepared with nonstick spray. When the bottom of the dish is covered, fry the rest of the batter in the same way and save it for topping.

3. In a bowl, mix the ricotta, 2 remaining eggs, Parmesan, vegetables, and parsley. Spread in tablespoonfuls over the base in the dish. Cover with more of the pasta strips.

4. Add the cream sauce to the dish and cover with shredded mozzarella. Bake for about 12 minutes. Serve hot.

Hawaiian-Style Rice with Pineapple, Mango, and Macadamia Nuts

This is perfect with grilled or roasted ham, pork chops, or pork tenderloin. Fruit blends well with the rice and is a fine side dish. You can also add crumbled crisp bacon as an interesting garnish.

INGREDIENTS | SERVES 4–6

1 cup water

1½ cups orange juice

1½ cups short-grain rice

Minced zest of 1 orange

1 teaspoon salt

Tabasco sauce, to taste

½ cup chopped pineapple

1 ripe mango, diced

2 tablespoons butter

½ cup toasted macadamia nuts, for garnish

1. Bring the water and juice to a boil. Stir in the rice and return to a boil. Cover and simmer for about 30 minutes or until the rice is tender.

2. Add the rest of the ingredients except the butter and nuts and reheat. Serve hot with butter and nuts arranged over the top.

Wild Rice Salad

This is just as good on a summer picnic as it is as a wintry side dish. It's filling and delightful.

INGREDIENTS | SERVES 6

4 cups water

¾ cup wild rice

Salt and black pepper, to taste

1 small red onion, chopped

3 stalks celery, rinsed and finely chopped

1 cup water chestnuts, drained and chopped

1 cup peeled, chopped jicama

1 small apple, cored and chopped

⅔ cup olive oil

⅓ cup raspberry vinegar

½ cup chopped fresh Italian flat-leaf parsley

6 ounces fresh raspberries

1. Bring water to a boil and add the rice; return to a rolling boil and then reduce heat to simmer and cover tightly. After 30 minutes, add salt and pepper.

2. When the rice has bloomed but is still hot, add the red onion, celery, water chestnuts, jicama, and apple. Taste and add more salt and pepper if desired.

3. Mix the olive oil and vinegar together with the parsley and combine with the rice and vegetables. Place in a large serving dish and serve warm or chilled. Sprinkle with berries at the last minute.

Cooking Wild Rice

Disregard the directions on the package of wild rice. They tell you to cook for 30–40 minutes, when it takes more like 90 minutes for it to bloom and soften. When cooking, just keep adding liquid if the rice dries out, and keep simmering until it "blooms" or the grains open up.

Spanish-Style Rice

This is an excellent side with a great steak. It can be made
in advance and then reheated just before serving time.

INGREDIENTS | SERVES 4

3 cups water

2 teaspoons salt

1 cup white rice

½ cup olive oil

1 large onion, chopped

1 clove garlic

2 jalapeño or poblano peppers, cored, seeded, and chopped

1 roasted red pepper, from a jar or your own, chopped

4 ripe plum tomatoes, cored and chopped

1 teaspoon lemon zest

10 black olives, sliced

Freshly ground black pepper, to taste

1. Bring the water to a boil and add the salt and the rice. Reduce the heat to a simmer, cover, and cook until tender, about 25 minutes.

2. While the rice is cooking, heat the oil in a large frying pan.

3. Add the onion, garlic, and hot peppers. Sauté over low heat for 8–10 minutes.

4. Mix in the rest of the ingredients and simmer for 10 minutes.

5. Thoroughly combine with the hot rice and serve.

Ground Pepper

You can get pink, white, and black peppercorns. Some cooks like to mix them. Some say there is a taste difference among the three. Other cooks use white pepper in white food so you won't see the black specks. Try a coarsely ground pepper in recipes like this one. To coarse-grind, place 6–8 peppercorns between two pieces of waxed paper. Use a heavy frying pan to press down on the corns until they are cracked and in coarse pieces. Don't just lay them on a board and hit them with the pan or they will fly all over the kitchen.

Confetti and Rice Pasta with Chicken

This is fun to eat and pretty to look at. The "confetti" is minced vegetables.
Lots of Parmesan cheese completes the dish.

INGREDIENTS | SERVES 4

½ cup olive oil

½ cup finely chopped red bell pepper

½ cup finely chopped yellow summer squash

1 bunch scallions, finely chopped

2 cloves garlic, finely chopped

½ cup brown rice flour

1 teaspoon salt

½ teaspoon pepper, or to taste

½ teaspoon dried thyme

¾ pound boneless, skinless chicken breast, cut into bite-size pieces

½ cup gluten-free chicken broth

8 ripe plum (Roma) tomatoes, or 1½ cups canned, chopped

1 teaspoon dried oregano

1 teaspoon dried basil

1 tablespoon red pepper flakes, or to taste

1 pound gluten-free brown rice pasta, cooked

1 cup freshly grated Parmesan cheese

1. Heat the olive oil and add the pepper, squash, scallions, and garlic. Sauté over medium heat, stirring frequently. While the vegetables are sautéing, mix the flour, salt, pepper, and thyme on a piece of waxed paper.

2. Dredge the chicken in the flour mixture and sauté along with the vegetables. Add the broth, tomatoes, oregano, basil, and red pepper flakes. Cook, uncovered, for 10 minutes to make sure the chicken is done.

3. Add the rice pasta to the pan and mix. Sprinkle with plenty of Parmesan cheese and serve.

Brown Rice Pasta

Rice pasta is available online through Amazon.com and through glutenfreemall.com. It's also becoming more readily available at most local grocery stores. Steer clear of soba noodles or "buckwheat" noodles. While buckwheat itself is actually in the rhubarb family and is gluten-free, most soba and buckwheat noodles contain wheat flour.

Classic Italian Risotto

*Risotto should be very creamy on the outside, with just a bit
of toothsome resistance on the inside of each grain of rice.*

INGREDIENTS | SERVES 4

5 cups canned or homemade gluten-free chicken or vegetable broth

2 tablespoons butter

2 tablespoons olive oil

½ cup finely chopped sweet onion

2 stalks celery, finely chopped

¼ cup chopped celery leaves

1½ cups Arborio rice

1 teaspoon salt, or to taste

⅔ cup freshly grated Parmesan cheese

¼ cup chopped parsley

Freshly ground black pepper, to taste

1. Bring the broth to a slow simmer over low heat and keep it hot.

2. Place the butter and oil in a heavy-bottomed pot over medium heat, melt butter, and add the onion, celery, and celery leaves. Cook for 8–10 minutes.

3. Add the rice and stir to coat with butter and oil. Stir in salt.

4. In ¼-cup increments, start adding hot broth and stir until the broth has been absorbed into the rice. Repeat this process until all of the hot broth is gone. It must be stirred constantly and takes about 35 minutes. (A stirring helper is nice.)

5. When all of the broth is gone, taste the rice. If it needs more broth or water, add it and keep stirring. Add the cheese, parsley, and pepper. Serve immediately.

Pumpkin and Bacon Risotto

*Many cooks love fresh pumpkin that is peeled, seeded, and cut up.
This saves endless time and energy. You can use a 15-ounce can of pumpkin purée instead
of fresh pumpkin if desired. This is a fine fall/winter side and is great with turkey.*

INGREDIENTS | SERVES 4

2 cups diced fresh pumpkin

Water to cover the pumpkin

1 tablespoon salt

4 strips bacon

5 cups canned or homemade gluten-free chicken broth

4 tablespoons butter

½ cup finely chopped sweet onion

2 teaspoons dried sage or 1 tablespoon chopped fresh

½ teaspoon dried oregano or 2 teaspoons chopped fresh

1½ cups Arborio rice

Salt and freshly ground black pepper, to taste

½ cup Parmesan cheese

¼ cup pepitas (pumpkin seeds), for garnish

Pumpkins Are High in Vitamin A

When you can get peeled, seeded, and chopped fresh pumpkin at the grocery store, go for it! Otherwise, it's easy to cut a pumpkin in half, remove the seeds, and place it cut-side down in a baking dish. Add ½" of water, cover with foil, and roast it for an hour or more in a 250°F oven. Then it's easy to purée. That is an excellent way to prepare pumpkin for pies and soups.

1. Put the diced pumpkin in a saucepan with water to cover and some salt. Simmer until the pumpkin is just tender, drain, and set aside, reserving the pumpkin liquid.

2. While the pumpkin is cooking, fry the bacon and drain it on paper towels. Crumble when cool. Heat the chicken broth in a large saucepan and keep at a low simmer.

3. Melt the butter in a big, heavy pot and add onion; sauté until soft. Add the sage, oregano, rice, and salt and pepper.

4. Slowly add the broth, ¼ cup at a time. When the pot hisses, add more broth. Repeat until broth is gone and then, if still dry, add some of the pumpkin liquid.

5. Stir in the pumpkin, Parmesan cheese, and bacon. Add extra pepper or butter if desired. Garnish with a sprinkle of pepitas and serve immediately.

Risotto with Radicchio and Gorgonzola Cheese

This is good as a side with poultry or seafood. It's also delicious on its own!

INGREDIENTS | SERVES 4

5 cups canned or homemade gluten-free chicken, fish, or vegetable broth

2 tablespoons butter

2 tablespoons olive oil

½ cup finely chopped sweet onion

1 head radicchio, rinsed and finely chopped

1½ cups Arborio rice

Salt and freshly ground black pepper, to taste

¼ cup crumbled Gorgonzola cheese

Roasted red pepper strips and chopped parsley, for garnish

1. Bring the broth to a slow simmer in a saucepan and keep hot.

2. Heat the butter and oil in a large, heavy pan; add the onion and radicchio and sauté until softened, about 8 minutes. Add the rice and stir. Add salt and pepper.

3. Add the broth, ¼ cup at a time, until it is all gone, stirring constantly. This will take about 35 minutes. If the risotto is still not done, add water, ¼ cup at a time.

4. When the rice is done, stir in the Gorgonzola cheese and garnish with strips of roasted red pepper and parsley. Serve hot.

Flavoring with Bacon

Bacon is an excellent garnish. It also can add flavor to soups and stews, and fat for sautéing vegetables, mushrooms, etc. A little goes a long way. If you are watching your diet, just drain the bacon well on paper towels and crumble it. Then, sprinkle it on soups, salads, vegetables, pasta, or rice.

Wild Rice with Dried Cranberries and Shallots

This is a great comfort good for when you're missing home.
Using beef broth instead of water will give this dish a stronger flavor.

INGREDIENTS | SERVES 6

4 cups water or gluten-free beef broth

¾ cup wild rice

1 teaspoon salt, or to taste

Freshly ground pepper, to taste

2 tablespoons butter

4 shallots, minced

2 tablespoons fresh rosemary or 1 tablespoon dried

½ cup dried cranberries, soaked in ⅔ cup port or other red wine for 30 minutes or until softened

Chopped celery tops, parsley, or other herbs, for garnish

1. Bring the water or broth to a boil and add the rice; return to a boil and lower heat to simmer. Add salt and pepper. Cover tightly and simmer until rice has bloomed. Check the rice for moisture and add liquid whenever necessary.

2. In a frying pan, melt the butter and add shallots; cook over medium heat until soft but not brown. Add the rosemary and remove from the heat.

3. When the rice is tender and bloomed, add the cooked shallots. Stir in the cranberries and port mixture. Taste and adjust seasonings if needed. Add garnish and serve warm or hot.

Steamed Jasmine Rice

Scented jasmine rice is a long-grain rice from Thailand that has a soft texture and a flavor similar to roasted nuts. Use it as a flavorful alternative to regular white rice.

INGREDIENTS | MAKES 3 CUPS

1¼ cups jasmine rice
1½ cups water

1. Rinse the rice, running your fingers through it to mix it around, until the water runs clear.

2. Bring the rice and water to a boil over medium heat. Reduce heat to low and cover tightly. Simmer until all the water is absorbed and the rice is cooked, 15–20 minutes.

3. Remove the pot from the heat. Do not remove the cover. Let the rice stand for 10–15 minutes. Fluff the rice with a fork and serve.

Pasta with Basil and Tomato Pesto

This recipe is designed to make extra sauce to save and serve with pasta on another night. To turn this into a dish for four, increase the amount of pasta to 3 cups and use all the sauce.

INGREDIENTS | SERVES 2

1½ cups gluten-free penne pasta (such as Heartland)
1 ounce fresh basil leaves
3 cloves garlic
1 large tomato
⅓ cup pine nuts
½ cup olive oil
½ cup grated Parmesan cheese

1. Cook the pasta in boiling salted water until tender but still firm (al dente). Drain.

2. Chop the basil leaves to make 1 cup. Smash, peel, and chop the garlic. Wash and chop the tomato, reserving the juice.

3. Process the garlic and pine nuts in a food processor. One at a time, add and process the basil leaves and tomato. Slowly add the olive oil and keep processing until the pesto is creamy. Add the Parmesan cheese. Pour half the pesto over the cooked pasta. Store the remaining pesto in a sealed container in the refrigerator for up to seven days.

Simple Vegetable Pasta

Warm your vegetables in a frying pan or in the microwave. If you prefer to cook them for a softer texture, use a frying pan and stir them until they are soft or slightly browned.

INGREDIENTS | SERVES 6

1 pound gluten-free spaghetti
10 ounces mixed frozen vegetables, thawed
1 teaspoon freshly grated rosemary
2 teaspoons minced onion
2 teaspoons minced garlic
Salt and pepper, to taste
¼ cup Parmesan cheese

1. Cook spaghetti according to package directions.

2. In a frying pan over medium heat, toss the mixed vegetables to warm them.

3. Mix rosemary, onion, garlic, and salt and pepper with the vegetables.

4. Pour vegetables over spaghetti and serve, sprinkling with cheese.

Shells with Zucchini

*Rosemary adds a rich depth of flavor to this simple summer pasta recipe,
and the Parmesan cheese topping adds just the right texture and taste. If you cannot locate
gluten-free pasta shells, use your favorite gluten-free pasta shape.*

INGREDIENTS | SERVES 4

1 tablespoon butter

2 cloves garlic, minced

3 zucchini, sliced

2 teaspoons minced fresh rosemary

¼ teaspoon salt

⅛ teaspoon white pepper

1 (12-ounce) package gluten-free pasta shells

3 tablespoons chopped flat-leaf parsley

¼ cup grated Parmesan cheese

1. Bring a large pot of water to a boil. In a large frying pan, melt butter over medium heat. Add garlic and zucchini and cook until crisp-tender, about 5–6 minutes. Add rosemary and salt and pepper. Cook for 2–3 minutes to blend flavors. Remove from heat.

2. Meanwhile, cook pasta in boiling salted water until al dente. Drain and add to zucchini mixture. Return to the heat and toss until the shells are coated with sauce, 2–3 minutes. Add the parsley and cheese and toss again. Serve immediately.

Cooking Pasta

Many chefs undercook pasta slightly and add it to the sauce in the pan. This way, the pasta absorbs flavors from the sauce. This is an important trick to remember when cooking gluten-free pasta. Many brands will overcook easily and it's best to generally boil the pasta for 6–8 minutes until "al dente," reserve some of the cooking liquid, and then drain the pasta. After draining the pasta, pour a tiny bit of olive oil and a little of the cooking liquid back over the noodles to keep them moist before serving. Remember that if you put pasta into a hot pan of sauce, it will continue to cook—be careful not to overcook and end up with mush!

Fresh Tomato with Angel Hair Pasta

This meal is simple but delicious. Throw in some leftover chicken or sausage if you want to add some protein and kick up the flavor a notch.

INGREDIENTS | SERVES 4–6

½ cup pine nuts

4 ripe beefsteak tomatoes

¼ cup extra-virgin olive oil

1 tablespoon lemon juice

¼ cup packed fresh basil leaves

½ teaspoon salt

⅛ teaspoon white pepper

1 pound gluten-free angel hair pasta

Fresh Basil

If you have a garden—or even just a sunny windowsill—by all means grow basil; it's easy to grow and requires very little maintenance. There are lots of kits available on the market or the Internet. Just be sure to use the basil before the plant starts to flower. You can also find fresh basil in the produce aisle of your supermarket.

1. Bring a large pot of water to a boil. Place a small frying pan over medium heat for 3 minutes. Add pine nuts; cook and stir for 3–5 minutes or until nuts begin to brown and are fragrant. Remove from heat and pour nuts into a large serving bowl.

2. Chop tomatoes into ½" pieces and add to pine nuts along with olive oil, lemon juice, basil, salt, and pepper. Add pasta to the boiling water; cook and stir until al dente, according to package directions. Drain and add to tomato mixture in bowl. Toss gently and serve immediately.

Herbed Rice Pilaf

The tiny thyme leaves will drop off the stem as the pilaf cooks,
adding a lemony-mint flavor to this easy recipe.

INGREDIENTS | SERVES 4

1 tablespoon olive oil

1 onion, chopped

2 stalks celery, chopped

2 cloves garlic, minced

1 fresh thyme sprig

½ teaspoon salt

⅛ teaspoon pepper

1 bay leaf

2½ cups water

1 cup long-grain brown rice

1. In a large saucepan, heat oil over medium heat. Add onion, celery, garlic, and thyme and sauté until onion is translucent, about 5 minutes. Add salt, pepper, bay leaf, and water, and bring to a boil.

2. Add rice, bring to a simmer, then cover, reduce heat to low, and simmer until all the water is absorbed and rice is tender, about 20 minutes. Remove and discard the bay leaf and the thyme stem; stir gently. Serve immediately.

Brown Rice and Spiced Peaches

This is great for a quick meal when you're jetting off to the library or class. You can prepare the rice and peaches in advance, mixing in milk and honey as desired, and heat in your microwave.

INGREDIENTS | SERVES 4

1 teaspoon salt

3 cups water

1½ cups brown rice

2 cups fresh or frozen peaches, or canned peaches in water (no syrup) with ¾ cup natural juices

½ teaspoon cinnamon

¼ teaspoon nutmeg

Juice of ½ lemon

2 teaspoons honey

1. Add salt to water and boil. Cook rice in salted water until tender, following package directions.

2. In a separate saucepan, mix peaches, cinnamon, nutmeg, lemon juice, and honey. Bring to a boil and set aside.

3. When ready to serve, mix the peaches and rice. Add warm milk and more honey if desired.

The Juice Solution

While it's always best to squeeze lemon or lime juice right out of the fruit, it's not always easy to keep fresh lemons and limes on hand. Luckily, you can buy bottles of lemon juice and lime juice that will stay good in the refrigerator for several weeks. These will come in handy in lots of recipes, from guacamole to fruit salad.

Penne with Pesto and Chicken

This dish is so delicious and quick to put together.
Share it with friends or save the rest for meals in a hurry.

INGREDIENTS | SERVES 8

1 (16-ounce) package gluten-free penne

2 tablespoons butter

2 tablespoons olive oil

4 skinless, boneless chicken breasts, cut into bite-size pieces

2 cloves garlic, minced

¾ cup gluten-free chicken broth

¾ cup milk

1 tablespoon cornstarch

Salt and black pepper, to taste

⅓ cup basil pesto (see sidebar for Pesto Potatoes in Chapter 8)

½ cup grated Parmesan cheese, divided

1 cup broccoli florets

Change Things Up

This dish is very versatile. If you do not like broccoli, simply substitute either asparagus or peas; both work great in this dish. Use your favorite gluten-free pasta. Pasta made from rice, corn, or quinoa all work wonderfully.

1. Bring a large pot of slightly salted water to a boil. Add pasta and cook according to package directions or until al dente. Drain and rinse pasta with hot water.

2. Heat butter and olive oil in a large frying pan over medium heat. Sauté chicken and garlic until chicken is almost cooked.

3. In a small bowl, stir together chicken broth, milk, and cornstarch. Pour into frying pan with chicken and garlic. Season to taste with salt and pepper.

4. Add pesto and half of the Parmesan cheese.

5. Add broccoli and cook until broccoli is tender. Stir in cooked pasta and toss to coat. Top with the remaining Parmesan cheese and serve.

Fettuccine Alfredo with Chicken

Ordering Italian food at a restaurant can be difficult when eating a gluten-free diet. Here is a restaurant-quality recipe you can make in your dorm. Add a tossed salad and a slice of gluten-free garlic toast, and your dinner is complete.

INGREDIENTS | SERVES 4

2 tablespoons olive oil

2 boneless, skinless chicken breasts

Salt and black pepper, to taste

8 ounces gluten-free fettuccine

½ cup (1 stick) butter

2 cloves garlic, minced

1 cup heavy cream

1 cup grated Parmesan cheese

1 tablespoon chopped fresh parsley (optional)

1. Heat olive oil in a small frying pan over medium-high heat. Cook chicken breasts until done, seasoning with salt and pepper.

2. Prepare gluten-free fettuccine according to package directions. Drain and set aside.

3. Add butter and garlic to the chicken. Once the butter has melted, add the heavy cream. Heat until the cream is starting to boil, and add the Parmesan cheese.

4. Reduce the heat to low and cook until the cheese is blended and the mixture begins to thicken.

5. Stir in the drained fettuccine, seasoning with more salt and pepper to taste. If desired, add fresh parsley before serving.

Baked Mexican Rice Casserole

This is a quick and easy dish you can get into the oven in just a few minutes.

INGREDIENTS | SERVES 4

1 (15-ounce) can black beans, drained and rinsed

¾ cup salsa

2 teaspoons chili powder

1 teaspoon cumin

½ cup corn kernels

2 cups cooked rice

½ cup grated Cheddar cheese

⅓ cup sliced black olives

1. Preheat the oven to 350°F.

2. Combine the beans, salsa, chili powder, and cumin in a large pot over low heat, and partially mash beans with a large fork.

3. Remove from heat and stir in corn and rice. Transfer to a casserole dish.

4. Top with cheese and olives and bake for 20 minutes.

Rice Pilaf

This side dish is perfect served alongside chicken, pork, or beef.

INGREDIENTS | SERVES 8

2 tablespoons olive oil

½ cup chopped onion

3 cloves garlic, minced

½ cup chopped celery

2 cups uncooked long-grain rice

1 teaspoon salt

⅛ teaspoon black pepper

4 cups gluten-free vegetable broth

2 tablespoons butter

Cooking Rice

For best results in cooking rice, first sauté the rice in a bit of oil until opaque. Then add water or broth, bring quickly to a boil, reduce heat, and cover. Don't uncover the rice as it cooks; just check it at the end of cooking time. Let the rice stand for a few minutes after cooking for fluffier rice with separate grains.

1. In heavy saucepan, combine olive oil, onion, garlic, and celery. Cook and stir over medium heat until crisp-tender, about 5 minutes.

2. Add rice; cook and stir 2 minutes longer. Sprinkle with salt and pepper and add broth.

3. Bring to a boil, then reduce heat to low, cover saucepan, and cook 15–20 minutes or until rice is tender and broth is absorbed. Remove from heat; add butter and let stand covered for 5 minutes. Fluff pilaf with fork and serve.

Fried Rice

*Fried rice doesn't have to contain egg! If you add some chicken
or ham to this easy recipe, you've created a main dish.*

INGREDIENTS | SERVES 6

¼ cup gluten-free vegetable broth

1 tablespoon gluten-free soy sauce (such as La Choy)

1 tablespoon minced fresh gingerroot

⅛ teaspoon ground black pepper

2 tablespoons olive oil

½ cup chopped onion

3 cloves garlic, minced

½ cup shredded carrot

½ cup chopped green onions

4 cups long-grain rice, cooked and cooled

1. In small bowl, combine broth, soy sauce, gingerroot, and pepper. Mix well and set aside.

2. In wok or large frying pan, heat olive oil over medium-high heat. Add onion and garlic; stir-fry 3 minutes. Add carrot and green onion; stir-fry 2–3 minutes longer.

3. Add rice and stir-fry until rice is hot and grains are separate, about 4–5 minutes. Stir broth mixture and add to wok; stir-fry until mixture bubbles, about 3–4 minutes. Serve immediately.

Try a Rice Cooker

If you have trouble cooking rice, get a rice cooker. This inexpensive appliance cooks rice to fluffy perfection every time. Another option is to cook rice like you cook pasta—in a large pot of boiling water. Keep tasting the rice; when it's tender, thoroughly drain and use in a recipe or serve.

CHAPTER 10

Special Occasions

Turkey Loaf

This can be served with rice or mashed potatoes on the side.
Depending on your desired spice level, you can make it milder as well.

INGREDIENTS | SERVES 4–6

1 pound ground turkey

1 cup blanched almond flour or gluten-free cornbread crumbs

⅔ cup milk

¼ cup chili sauce

3 eggs

1 teaspoon thyme

½ cup chopped onion

Salt and pepper, to taste

¼ teaspoon nutmeg

4 strips of bacon

1. Preheat the oven to 350°F.

2. Put all the ingredients except the bacon into your food processor and process until well blended.

3. Pour into a 9" × 5" loaf pan and put that pan into a much larger one (such as an 11" × 13" pan). Place in the oven and add boiling water to the larger pan. Cut the bacon in halves and arrange across the top of the loaf. Bake for 1 hour.

4. Serve with mashed potatoes.

Stuffing for Roasted Turkey

*Make your own gluten-free cornbread for stuffing a day or two before,
cube, and place in the refrigerator in a plastic bag until ready to use.*

**INGREDIENTS | MAKES STUFFING FOR 1
TURKEY**

1 onion, finely chopped

4 stalks celery with tops, finely chopped

4 tablespoons butter

1 pound bulk breakfast sausage

10 cups cubed gluten-free cornbread

1 cup (2 sticks) unsalted butter, melted
with ½ cup water

2 teaspoons dried thyme

10 fresh sage leaves, minced, or 2
tablespoons dried

2 large tart apples, peeled, cored, and
chopped

Salt and pepper, to taste

1. In a large frying pan, sauté the onion and celery in the butter over medium heat for about 5 minutes. Add the sausage and break up with a wooden spoon. Cook until sausage is done and vegetables are tender, about 10 minutes. Place in a very large bowl.

2. Add the rest of the ingredients to the bowl. With your hands inside large plastic bags, use your hands to mix the ingredients well. Stuff your turkey with this mixture.

The Best Roasted Turkey

For the sweetest, juiciest bird, try to find a turkey that is between 9 and 12 pounds.
Make extra gravy by adding a can of chicken broth to the basting liquid.

INGREDIENTS | SERVES 15

1 (10-pound) turkey

¼ pound (1 stick) butter, softened

1 teaspoon dried thyme

½ cup minced fresh Italian flat-leaf parsley

Salt, to taste

1 teaspoon pepper

Giblets, including wing tips and neck

½ cup dry white wine

Water for cooking

2 bay leaves

1 recipe Stuffing for Roasted Turkey (see this chapter)

4 strips bacon for bottom of roasting pan

2 teaspoons cornstarch

¼ cup water

Roasting Turkeys

Always start the turkey breast-side down so the juices run into, rather than out of, the breast. The bacon prevents the breast from sticking to the roasting pan and adds a nice flavor to the juices. If, like most families, yours likes extra stuffing, make 3 to 4 cups extra and roast it in a casserole dish while you are roasting the turkey.

1. Rinse the turkey in cold water and pat dry. Thoroughly mix the butter, herbs, salt, and pepper and tease mixture under the skin of the breast, working it into the thighs. Be careful not to tear the skin.

2. Place the giblets and wing tips in a saucepan with the wine and water to cover. Add the bay leaves. Cook for 2 hours, or while the turkey is cooking. Add extra water if the liquid gets too low.

3. Stuff the turkey with stuffing and skewer the legs together. Close the neck cavity with a skewer. Preheat the oven to 325°F.

4. Place the bacon on the bottom of the roasting pan and start the turkey breast-side down. After 30 minutes, turn over the turkey and arrange the bacon over the breast and legs. Roast for 3 hours, basting every 20 minutes with the giblet liquid, then with the pan juices. Roast until the thickest part is 155°F on a meat thermometer. Let the turkey rest for 15 minutes before carving.

5. Make gravy by mixing 2 teaspoons cornstarch with ¼ cup water and blending with pan juices.

The Best Meatloaf

*This is classic comfort food. With some mashed potatoes and gravy,
you won't want to go to the dining hall for dinner.*

INGREDIENTS | SERVES 6–8

1½ pounds ground beef, either chuck or sirloin

½ cup chili sauce

½ cup milk

3 eggs

1 cup gluten-free cornbread crumbs

Salt and pepper, to taste

2 cloves garlic, minced

1 small onion, minced

1 teaspoon crumbled dried rosemary

2 teaspoons gluten-free steak sauce (such as Lea & Perrins)

½ teaspoon nutmeg

A Hot Water Bath

Baking your meat loaf in a hot water bath enables it to stay juicy. Processing the ingredients makes a much smoother meat-loaf than the coarse stuff that you have to chew for a long time. The water bath is called a bain-marie, and it keeps baked foods soft, creamy, and moist.

1. Preheat the oven to 350°F.

2. In the large bowl of a food processor, process all the ingredients together. If you don't have a food processor, simply mix all of the ingredients in a large bowl using a wooden spoon or your hands.

3. Prepare a 9" × 5" loaf pan with nonstick spray. Pour in the meatloaf mixture.

4. Place a roasting pan in the middle of the oven. Add 1" of water. Place the loaf pan with the meatloaf in the water. Bake for 1 hour and 20 minutes. For an extra touch, drape 2 slices of bacon over the top of the meatloaf before baking.

Light Gorgonzola and Ricotta Torte Appetizer

*This is light and delicious. You will find that this works best in
a springform pan. Serve warm or at room temperature.*

INGREDIENTS | SERVES 6

16 ounces fresh whole-milk ricotta
cheese

4 ounces Gorgonzola cheese, crumbled

1 teaspoon fresh oregano, or ¼
teaspoon dried

1 teaspoon fresh lemon juice

1 teaspoon freshly grated lemon zest

Salt and pepper, to taste

3 egg whites, beaten stiff

½ cup chopped and toasted hazelnuts,
for garnish

1. Preheat the oven to 350°F.

2. Process the cheeses, oregano, lemon juice, lemon zest, and salt and pepper in a food processor until very smooth. Place in a bowl and fold in the egg whites.

3. Spray the inside of a 10" springform pan. Add the cheese mixture and bake for abut 30 minutes or until slightly golden.

4. Sprinkle with hazelnuts. Cool slightly and serve in wedges.

The Ties That Bind

Gluten is the "glue" that holds breads, cakes, and piecrusts together. When you substitute gluten-free flours for gluten-containing flours, you generally need to use eggs or other stabilizers such as guar gum or xanthan gum to hold things together. As more and more people have learned to cook and bake gluten-free, they have discovered more natural ingredients that also help stabilize gluten-free baked goods, such as chia seeds, flaxseeds, and psyllium husks.

Savory Chicken Spread

You can use leftover roast chicken or turkey for an excellent substitution.
This works nicely as a stuffing for celery or a spread for crackers.

INGREDIENTS | MAKES 3 CUPS

2 cups cooked chicken (white or dark meat)

1 stalk celery, coarsely chopped

1 or 2 scallions, white parts peeled

2 shallots, peeled

⅔ cup mayonnaise (not low-fat)

1 teaspoon Madras curry powder

1 teaspoon Dijon mustard

1 teaspoon dried thyme

½ teaspoon celery salt

Salt and freshly ground black pepper, to taste

½ cup chopped fresh parsley

1. Place all the ingredients in a food processor and process until coarsely blended.

2. Scrape into an attractive bowl and chill until ready to serve. Try with toasted gluten-free baguette slices, chips, or on lettuce as a first course. Possible garnishes include chopped chives, capers, sliced green or black olives, or baby gherkin pickles.

Shirred Eggs and Asparagus au Gratin

This is a very easy brunch or supper dish. You can use frozen asparagus, but fresh is better. The trick is arranging the asparagus evenly in the pan.

INGREDIENTS | SERVES 4

1 pound fresh asparagus, ends trimmed, or 2 (10-ounce) packages frozen

8 eggs

1 cup crumbled Roquefort cheese

1. Blanch the asparagus in boiling water for 5 minutes. Shock in ice water and drain.

2. Preheat the oven to 350°F. Prepare a gratin pan or casserole dish with nonstick spray.

3. Arrange the asparagus on the bottom of the pan. Break the eggs over the top.

4. Sprinkle with Roquefort and bake until eggs are done and cheese is hot and runny, about 12 minutes. Serve hot.

Tasty Turkey Parmesan

You can doctor your sauce with extra herbs and some lemon zest for more complex flavors.

INGREDIENTS | SERVES 4

1¼ pounds boneless, skinless turkey breast, thinly sliced

1 cup gluten-free cornbread crumbs

1 cup Parmesan cheese, divided

Salt and pepper, to taste

1 cup brown rice flour

1 egg, beaten

1 cup oil for frying

2 cups tomato sauce

½ pound whole-milk mozzarella, shredded or thinly sliced

What's in the Stuffing?

The key to buying gluten-free food is reading every label carefully. Store-bought cornbread stuffing may have wheat flour mixed in with the corn flour and cornmeal. Corn muffins, also a favorite in making homemade stuffing, can have a mixture of wheat flour and cornmeal. In the long run, the safest way to provide gluten-free stuffing is to make the cornbread yourself.

1. Flatten the turkey breast with a meat tenderizer. Cut into four pieces. Mix the cornbread crumbs with ½ cup of the Parmesan cheese and salt and pepper. Dip the turkey in the brown rice flour, then in the egg, and finally in the crumb mixture.

2. Preheat the oven to 350°F. Prepare a baking dish with nonstick spray.

3. In a frying pan over medium heat, fry the turkey in oil until golden brown. Drain on paper towels.

4. Pour a little tomato sauce into the baking dish. Add the turkey pieces. Sprinkle with remaining ½ cup Parmesan cheese. Cover with tomato sauce. Spread the mozzarella over the top.

5. Bake until hot and bubbling, about 20 minutes. Serve hot.

Fruit and Corn-Crusted Pork Tenderloin

This is a perfect dish to make when Mom and Dad come to visit. It is easy and has a ton of flavor.

INGREDIENTS | SERVES 4–6

6 dried apricots, chopped
½ cup dried cranberries
¼ cup golden raisins
1 cup warm water
Juice of ½ lemon
2 pork tenderloins, about ¾ pound each
Gluten-free Worcestershire sauce to taste
1 cup gluten-free cornmeal (such as Bob's Red Mill)
1 teaspoon salt
Freshly ground black pepper, to taste
½ cup olive oil

1. Put the dried fruit in a bowl with the warm water and lemon juice. Let stand until most of the water is absorbed.

2. Preheat the oven to 350°F.

3. Make a tunnel through each tenderloin using a fat knitting needle or the handle of a blunt knife. Stuff the fruit into the tunnels.

4. Sprinkle both tenderloins with Worcestershire sauce.

5. In a small bowl, make a paste with the cornmeal, salt, pepper, and olive oil. Spread it on the pork.

6. Roast the pork for 30 minutes. The crust should be golden brown and the pork pink.

Shrimp and Lobster Salad

Try using different citrus fruits and mixing in different vegetables.
Use almonds instead of peanuts. And if you like cilantro, use that instead of parsley.

INGREDIENTS | SERVES 4

1 cup mayonnaise

1 teaspoon Dijon mustard

Juice of ½ lime and 1 teaspoon zest

1 teaspoon gluten-free soy sauce (such as La Choy)

1 tablespoon chili sauce

1 teaspoon minced garlic

Salt and pepper, to taste

Meat of 1 small (1½-pound) lobster, cooked

½ pound cleaned and cooked shrimp

¼ cup snipped fresh dill weed and chopped fresh parsley, mixed

1 tablespoon capers

4 lettuce leaves, shredded

1. In a medium bowl, mix together the mayonnaise, mustard, lime juice and zest, soy sauce, chili sauce, garlic, and salt and pepper.

2. Just before serving, mix the sauce with the seafood. Garnish with snipped fresh dill weed and chopped parsley, sprinkle with capers, and serve over a bed of lettuce.

Capers

These tiny berries are pickled in brine or packed in salt. The islands of the Mediterranean are lush with the bushes that produce them, and they are used in profusion in many fish, meat, and salad dishes. The French love them, as do the Italians, Greeks, Sardinians, and Maltese. Try some in a butter sauce over a piece of fresh striped bass and you'll understand their popularity.

Roasted Cornish Game Hens with Ginger-Orange Glaze

*This recipe is a snap and tastes wonderful. When the spring rolls around,
this will make a delicious, but sticky, picnic.*

INGREDIENTS | SERVES 4

2 Cornish game hens, split

2 tablespoons olive oil

Generous sprinkle of salt and pepper

1 tablespoon orange marmalade

2 tablespoons peanut oil

1 tablespoon gluten-free soy sauce (such as La Choy)

2 tablespoons orange juice

1 tablespoon minced fresh gingerroot

Fresh Gingerroot

You can use fresh gingerroot in all kinds of dishes, from dinners to desserts. Dried ground ginger, ginger snaps, and candied ginger are often used in cooking. Unpeeled fresh ginger freezes beautifully and can be added to sauces, salad dressings, and desserts such as puddings. When you want to use it, cut off an inch or two and peel it; then grate it, mince it, or finely chop it.

1. Preheat the oven to 375°F.

2. Rinse the hens, pat dry with paper towels, brush with olive oil, and sprinkle with salt and pepper.

3. Stir the rest of the ingredients together in a small saucepan over low heat to make glaze; set aside.

4. Roast hens in a baking dish or pan, cut-side up, for 15 minutes. Turn hens and brush with glaze. Continue to roast for another 20 minutes, brushing hens with glaze every 5 minutes.

Mexican-Style Corn Tortillas Stuffed with Shrimp and Avocado

This is a great lunch or brunch dish on a hot day. Not to mention, your friends will love it.

INGREDIENTS | MAKES 6 TORTILLAS

6 gluten-free corn tortillas or 6 Brown Rice Crepes (see Chapter 2)

24 extra-large shrimp, peeled and deveined

½ cup dry white wine

6 medium avocados, pitted, peeled, and sliced

1 red onion, thinly sliced

Juice of 2 fresh limes

1 teaspoon freshly ground coriander

1 tablespoon red pepper flakes

1 cup fresh or jarred salsa

1 cup sour cream

½ cup chopped cilantro or parsley

1. Warm the tortillas or crepes and place on serving plates.

2. Poach the cleaned shrimp in the white wine and drain.

3. Stack 4 shrimp on each tortilla, add the avocado and onion, and sprinkle with lime juice, coriander, and pepper flakes.

4. Spoon salsa over each tortilla, add a dollop of sour cream, and garnish with either cilantro or parsley.

Finding the Perfect Gluten-Free Wrap

You can make gluten-free corn tortillas using masa harina—the only hard part is getting them to be thin and crisp as opposed to thick and hard to eat. Serious Latin cooks buy a press to stamp out their tortillas. Another option to is try gluten-free "flour" tortillas; there are a few types available by Rudi's brand and Food For Life brand (brown rice tortillas). They can be found at most health-food stores in the freezer section.

Lobster Tails with Butter

*Always place the lobster approximately 4 inches away from the
heat source, no matter what method you are using to cook it.*

INGREDIENTS | SERVES 2

2 (5-ounce) rock lobster tails, fresh or frozen
⅓ cup butter
1 tablespoon, plus 1 teaspoon, clam juice

1. Preheat broiler. If using frozen lobster tails, thaw and pat dry with paper towels.

2. Melt the butter in a small saucepan over medium-low heat. Add the clam juice. Simmer for 5 minutes and remove from the heat.

3. Use scissors to cut lengthwise through the top of the lobster shell. Cut through the meat almost to the bottom, but do not cut right through the soft bottom shell. Use your hands to gently push apart the meat on both sides of the cut.

4. Lightly brush the lobster with a small amount of the butter mixture. Broil for 10–15 minutes, until cooked but still tender. Halfway through cooking, brush again with the butter. Serve the lobster tails with the remaining butter mixture.

Aloha Grilled Shrimp

For best results, cover the shrimp and chill for 2 hours before cooking.

INGREDIENTS | SERVES 2

1 pound shrimp, peeled and deveined

½ red bell pepper

⅓ cup gluten-free soy sauce (such as La Choy)

1 tablespoon cooking sherry

2 teaspoons brown sugar

1 cup pineapple chunks, drained

1. Rinse the shrimp by letting them stand in warm salted water for 5 minutes. Pat dry with paper towels.

2. Wash the red pepper, remove the seeds, and cut into small chunks. Combine the soy sauce, cooking sherry, and brown sugar in a small bowl.

3. Preheat grill or oven broiler. Fill two metal skewers with three or four shrimp apiece, alternating them with a piece of red pepper and a chunks of pineapple. Brush the sauce over the kebabs. Grill or broil for 5–8 minutes, turning occasionally and brushing with more sauce until the shrimp are opaque throughout.

Quick and Easy Beef Medallions with Fiddlehead Greens

The earthy flavor, bright green color, and unusual rolled shape of fiddlehead greens make them a nice complement to beef medallions. If you can't find fiddlehead greens, use fresh or frozen asparagus instead.

INGREDIENTS | SERVES 2

2 teaspoons freshly ground black pepper, or to taste

6 (3-ounce) beef medallions

2 cloves garlic

4 tablespoons olive oil, divided

1½ cups chicken broth

8 ounces frozen fiddlehead greens

Freezing Tip

Always be sure to label frozen food with the date that it is frozen. Although frozen food has a longer storage period than refrigerated food, it will eventually go bad. Labeling food with the freezing date means you're not relying on memory to know if it is still edible.

1. Rub the freshly ground black pepper over the beef medallions. Set aside. Smash, peel, and chop the garlic cloves.

2. Heat 2 tablespoons of the olive oil in a frying pan on medium-low heat. Add the beef medallions. Cook for 3–4 minutes on each side, until both sides are thoroughly browned. Remove from the pan and clean out the frying pan.

3. Add the remaining 2 tablespoons olive oil. Add the garlic. Cook for 1 minute, then add the chicken broth.

4. Add the fiddlehead greens. Cook for 4–5 minutes or until the greens are heated through. Return the beef medallions to the pan. Heat through and serve hot.

Baked Ham with Soy Glaze

This is a great recipe for those occasions when you want to entertain your parents instead of being stuck in the kitchen cooking. Serve with Baked Potato (see Chapter 6).

INGREDIENTS | SERVES 4

2 tablespoons gluten-free soy sauce (such as La Choy)

1 teaspoon honey mustard

2 teaspoons brown sugar

1 teaspoon pineapple juice

1 (3-pound) precooked ham

1. Preheat the oven to 325°F.

2. In a small bowl, combine the soy sauce, honey mustard, brown sugar, and pineapple juice to make the glaze.

3. Place the ham in a shallow dish and baste with the glaze.

4. Bake for 45 minutes, brushing with the glaze several times during the cooking process.

Red Snapper with Vegetables

Red snapper goes well with simple vegetable dishes. Steamed rice also makes a nice accompaniment.

INGREDIENTS | SERVES 4

4 red snapper fillets
3 pearl onions
¼ cup extra-virgin olive oil
1 tablespoon lemon juice
2 tomatoes

1. Rinse the fish fillets and pat dry. Place the fillets in a shallow glass baking dish.

2. Peel and chop the pearl onions.

3. In a small bowl, combine the olive oil and the lemon juice. Pour the marinade over the fish. Add the pearl onions. Marinate the fish for 30 minutes in the refrigerator.

4. While the fish is marinating, preheat the oven to 375°F.

5. Cut the tomatoes into wedges. Remove the fish from the refrigerator and add the tomatoes to the dish.

6. Bake the fish for 20 minutes or until opaque (a milky color) throughout.

Gourmet Chili

For a different flavor, try replacing 1 cup of the kidney beans with canned chickpeas or black-eyed peas.

INGREDIENTS | SERVES 4

1½ pounds sirloin steak

½ small white onion

½ red bell pepper

2 tablespoons vegetable oil

1 tablespoon chili powder, or to taste

½ teaspoon ground cumin

½ teaspoon garlic powder

2 cups canned kidney beans, with juice

2 cups crushed tomatoes

Healthy Legumes

Beans and peas are a dieter's dream. Besides being low in fat and high in complex carbohydrates, starchy legumes like black-eyed peas, kidney beans, and lima beans are a good source of B vitamins and important minerals such as zinc. Use them in soups and salads, or as a side dish or a protein-packed alternative to meat at a main meal.

1. Cut the meat into bite-size cubes, about 1" thick. Wash and dry the vegetables. Peel and chop the onion. Remove the seeds from the red pepper and chop.

2. Heat the oil in a frying pan over medium-low heat. Add the onion and red pepper. Sauté until the onion is tender, about 5 minutes.

3. Add the meat and cook over medium-high heat until browned, about 8–10 minutes. Do not drain. Stir in the chili powder, ground cumin, and garlic powder. Mix in the kidney beans and the crushed tomatoes.

4. Cover the chili and simmer over low heat for about 45 minutes. Serve hot with rice or bread.

Irish Stew

Lamb is traditionally used to make Irish stew, but you can substitute stewing beef if desired.

INGREDIENTS | SERVES 4

2 white onions

2 parsnips

4 red new potatoes

2 tablespoons vegetable oil

1½ pounds lean boneless lamb, cut into cubes for stewing

3 cups low-sodium, gluten-free chicken broth

2 sprigs chopped fresh parsley

¼ teaspoon celery salt, or to taste

Salt and pepper, to taste

1. Peel and chop the onions. Wash and peel the parsnips and potatoes. Dice the parsnips and cut the potatoes into chunks.

2. Heat the vegetable oil in a large, heavy saucepan. Add half the onion and cook until lightly browned.

3. Add half the lamb and cook until browned. Remove from the saucepan. Cook the remaining lamb in the pan, adding more oil if necessary. Return the first batch of cooked meat to the pan.

4. Add the chicken broth, parsley, celery salt, and salt and pepper. Bring to a boil. Reduce heat to low, cover, and simmer for 45 minutes.

5. Add the potatoes and parsnips. Simmer for 15 more minutes, then add the remaining onion. Simmer for another 15 minutes or until the potatoes and parsnips are tender.

One-Step Roast Chicken

Once you've mastered the basic skill of roasting chicken, you may want to try a few creative variations, such as placing lemon slices underneath the skin.

INGREDIENTS | SERVES 4

1 (3½–5-pound) fryer chicken
1½ tablespoons olive oil
2 teaspoons dried rosemary
2 teaspoons dried thyme

1. Preheat the oven to 375°F.

2. Rinse the chicken under cold, running water and pat dry. Rub the olive oil, dried rosemary, and dried thyme over the chicken. Place the chicken on the rack in a shallow roasting pan. Bake for 1 hour or until the juices run clear when the chicken is pricked with a fork. If checking doneness with a meat thermometer, the internal temperature of the chicken should be at least 175° at the thickest part of the thigh.

Sweet Potato Apple Purée

*Now this is a dish for the holidays! Serve it by itself or as a sauce
for turkey, stuffing, and other Thanksgiving favorites.*

INGREDIENTS | SERVES 12

3 pounds sweet potatoes, peeled and cubed

2 Granny Smith apples, peeled and cubed

½ cup apple juice

2 tablespoons butter

½ teaspoon ground nutmeg

1 teaspoon salt

¼ teaspoon white pepper

¼ cup toasted sunflower seeds

1. Place potatoes in a large saucepan and cover with water. Cover saucepan, bring to a boil, reduce the heat to medium-low, and cook until tender, about 15 minutes. Drain.

2. Meanwhile, in a small saucepan, combine the apples with apple juice. Bring to a simmer over medium heat and cook until tender, about 5 minutes.

3. Transfer potatoes and apples with liquid to a food processor. Add butter, nutmeg, salt, and pepper and purée until smooth. Sprinkle with sunflower seeds and serve.

Coriander Carrots

Carrots make a wonderful side dish, and these are especially fragrant and flavorful.

INGREDIENTS | SERVES 6

1 tablespoon olive oil

1 onion, chopped

1 cup water

1 bay leaf

½ teaspoon salt

1½ pounds carrots, thickly sliced

¼ cup dried currants

1 tablespoon butter

2 teaspoons ground coriander

2 tablespoons lemon juice

3 tablespoons minced flat-leaf parsley

Serve 'Em Up Right

Coriander and bay leaf add a nice spicy touch to tender carrots. Serve this carrot dish with grilled chicken or rice dishes, or as a side for your Thanksgiving meal.

1. Heat oil in a large saucepan over medium heat. Add onion; cook and stir until crisp-tender, about 4 minutes. Add water, bay leaf, salt, carrots, and currants and bring to a simmer.

2. Cover pan, reduce heat to low, and simmer for 10–15 minutes or until carrots are tender when tested with a fork.

3. Drain carrots, removing bay leaf, and return saucepan to heat. Add butter, coriander, lemon juice, and parsley; cook and stir over low heat for 2–3 minutes or until carrots are glazed. Serve immediately.

Mulled Spiced Cider

This is a classic holiday drink. Serve nice and hot on a chilly fall day or winter's night.

INGREDIENTS | MAKES 1 QUART

28 ounces apple cider
Juice of 1 lemon
1 orange, thinly sliced and seeded
10 whole cloves
2 cinnamon sticks
½ teaspoon whole allspice

Mix all the ingredients together, heat to desired temperature, and serve.

Chestnut Purée

This is a wonderful accompaniment to holiday meats like turkey, game hens, or duck. If you use chestnuts from a can or a jar, you will save a great deal of time.

INGREDIENTS | MAKES 1 CUP

8 ounces chestnuts, shelled
Salt and pepper, to taste
Pinch nutmeg
½ cup whole milk or light cream

Purée all the ingredients in a blender or food processor. Warm over low heat and serve.

Charming Chestnuts

While your R.A. probably wouldn't want you roasting these over an open fire, you can still enjoy this classic holiday food while at college. Chestnuts contain very little fat and no gluten, and they're the only nut that has any vitamin C, so they're a great choice for a snack or for use in a recipe.

Baked Sweet Potato Fries

*Tired of the same old sweet potatoes at Thanksgiving? Give these sweet,
crispy fries a try! Once your friends catch a whiff, you'll have a holiday party in no time!*

INGREDIENTS | SERVES 6

2 pounds sweet potatoes, peeled
2 teaspoons ground cinnamon
1 tablespoon olive oil

1. Preheat the oven to 450°F. Cut potatoes into sticks, about ½" thick. Toss potatoes, cinnamon, and olive oil in a bowl.

2. Coat a large cookie sheet with nonstick spray. Bake for 25–30 minutes or until potatoes are fairly crispy.

Salmon Spinach Salad

*This salad makes perfect use of leftover salmon! Salmon will only remain good
in the fridge for two days, so make sure you find a good use for it quickly!*

INGREDIENTS | SERVES 1

1 (5-ounce) salmon fillet, cooked
1 cup spinach leaves
½ cup red grapes
¼ cup shredded carrots
½ tablespoon sliced almonds
1 tablespoon dried cranberries

Combine all the ingredients in a bowl and enjoy!

Hash Brown Casserole

This recipe makes a huge amount, so it's perfect for entertaining or holidays.

1 (32-ounce) package frozen hash browns, thawed and drained of liquids

½ cup minced onion

2 cloves garlic, minced

1 teaspoon salt

¼ teaspoon ground black pepper

1 cup cream cheese, softened

⅓ cup milk

2 cups shredded mozzarella cheese

1. Preheat the oven to 375°F. Spray a 13" × 9" baking dish with nonstick cooking spray and set aside.

2. In a large bowl, combine all the ingredients and mix well.

3. Spoon the mixture into a baking dish and spread into an even layer. Cover and bake for 30 minutes, then uncover and bake 30–40 minutes longer or until casserole is bubbly and starting to brown. Serve immediately.

Hash Browns

You can find hash browns in the refrigerated and freezer sections of your local grocery store. Read labels carefully, as some brands do contain gluten. To thaw the frozen potatoes, just let the bag stand in the refrigerator overnight. Drain the potatoes well before using in recipes.

Gazpacho

Gazpacho is best made the day before so that the flavors will penetrate all the vegetables. It should be served chilled.

INGREDIENTS | SERVES 6

1 (28-ounce) can no-salt-added chopped tomatoes

1 green bell pepper, chopped

3 medium tomatoes, peeled and chopped

1 cucumber, peeled and chopped

1 small onion, chopped

2 tablespoons olive oil

½ teaspoon black pepper

½ teaspoon paprika

¼ teaspoon cayenne pepper

1 teaspoon chopped chives

2 teaspoons chopped parsley

½ clove garlic, minced

4½ teaspoons lemon juice

1. Blend canned tomatoes in blender until smooth. Pour into a large bowl.

2. Add the remaining ingredients to the bowl and stir to combine.

3. Refrigerate for at least 12 hours, then serve.

Spiced Tea

This tea can be served hot or over ice. You can change the flavor quite easily with different tea bag flavors. It's a perfect accompaniment to long nights in the library.

INGREDIENTS | SERVES 6

4 bags herbal tea

1 teaspoon ground nutmeg

½ teaspoon ground cinnamon

¼ teaspoon ground cloves

6 cups boiling water

1. In a ceramic teapot, combine the teabags and spices.

2. Pour boiling water into teapot. Steep for 5 minutes, then remove teabags.

CHAPTER 11

Desserts

Baked Ricotta Torte with Candied Orange Peel and Chocolate Chips

This dessert is rich and a very easy to make for a group of friends or visiting family members.

INGREDIENTS | SERVES 6–8

5 eggs

1 pound whole-milk ricotta cheese

4 ounces cream cheese (not low- or nonfat)

1 teaspoon vanilla extract

1 teaspoon salt

¾ cup chopped candied orange peel

1 cup chocolate bits or semisweet chocolate chips

1. Preheat the oven to 350°F. Separate the eggs and beat the whites until stiff. Set aside. Put the yolks, cheeses, vanilla, and salt in the food processor and process until smooth.

2. Place in a bowl and fold in the egg whites, candied orange peel, and chocolate bits or chips. Prepare a pie plate (preferably glass) with nonstick spray. Pour in the egg mixture and bake for 45 minutes or until set and golden on top.

Ricotta Cheese and Cottage Cheese

You can substitute cottage cheese for ricotta in any recipe. Just be sure to use the small-curd, low-salt variety. Cottage cheese may be a bit moister than ricotta—you can drain it by using a sieve and letting the fluid run out, or you can wring it out in cheesecloth.

Chocolate Mint Swirl Cheesecake
with Chocolate Nut Crust

This is incredibly rich and delicious. It is definitely a special-occasion cake with layers of deep flavor. Because it is so decadent, cut the pieces small when serving.

INGREDIENTS | SERVES 10–12

1½ cups ground walnuts (the food processor works well)

½ cup sugar

⅓ cup unsalted butter, melted

4 ounces semisweet chocolate, melted

4 eggs, separated

3 (8-ounce) packages cream cheese (not low- or nonfat)

1 cup sour cream

¾ cup sugar

1½ teaspoons vanilla extract

1 teaspoon salt

2 tablespoons arrowroot starch or tapioca starch

4 ounces semisweet chocolate

2 tablespoons peppermint schnapps

Whipped cream, for topping (optional)

Baking with Cream Cheese

It's best to use cream cheese that is not low- or nonfat. The lower the fat content, the more chemicals there are in the cheese to make it work for spreading. When baking, use the purest ingredients, as heat will change the consistency of anything artificial.

1. Mix the first four ingredients together. Prepare a 9" × 9" springform pan with nonstick spray and press the walnut mixture into the bottom to make a crust. Chill for at least 1 hour.

2. Preheat the oven to 350°F. In a clean bowl, beat the egg whites until stiff. In a separate bowl, using an electric mixer, beat the cream cheese, sour cream, sugar, vanilla, salt, and starch in a large bowl. Melt the semisweet chocolate with the schnapps.

3. With the electric mixer running, add the egg yolks, one at a time, beating vigorously. Fold in the stiff egg whites. Using a knife, swirl the chocolate and schnapps into the bowl.

4. Pour into the prepared springform pan and bake for 1 hour. Turn off the oven, and with the door cracked, let the cake cool for another hour. Chill before serving. Add whipped cream to the top before serving if desired.

Cherry Vanilla Cheesecake with Walnut Crust

This is a fine combination with a delightful flavor and smooth consistency.

INGREDIENTS | SERVES 10–12

1½ cups ground walnuts

½ cup sugar

½ cup (1 stick) unsalted butter, melted

4 eggs, separated

3 (8-ounce) packages cream cheese

1 cup sour cream

2 teaspoons vanilla extract

1 teaspoon salt

2 tablespoons brown rice flour

⅔ cup cherry preserves, melted

Nut Crusts for Cheesecake

This recipe specifies walnuts because they are probably the least expensive shelled nut and work well in these recipes. However, you can substitute hazelnuts, almonds, or pecans. Pecans add a Southern touch and are really good but expensive. Grinding nuts is simple—just use your food processor.

1. Mix together the walnuts, sugar, and butter. Prepare a springform pan with nonstick spray and press the nut mixture into the bottom to form a crust. Chill for at least 1 hour.

2. Preheat the oven to 350°F.

3. Beat the egg whites and set aside.

4. In a large bowl, using an electric mixer, beat the cream cheese, sour cream, vanilla, salt, and brown rice flour together.

5. Add the egg yolks, one at a time, while beating. When smooth, fold in the egg whites and mix in the cherry preserves.

6. Pour into prepared springform pan and bake for 1 hour. Turn off oven and crack the door. Let cake cool for another hour. Chill before serving.

Lemon Cheesecake with Nut Crust

This cheesecake is light, with an intense lemon flavor. It's a good summer cheesecake that will make your guests ask for more.

INGREDIENTS | SERVES 10–12

1¼ cups ground walnuts (or whatever nuts you like)

½ cup sugar

½ cup (1 stick) unsalted butter, melted

5 egg whites

3 (8-ounce) packages cream cheese

1 cup sour cream

⅔ cup sugar

2 tablespoons brown rice flour

1 teaspoon salt

3 egg yolks

Juice of 1 lemon

Minced rind of 1 lemon

Extra nuts and paper-thin lemon slices, to garnish cake

Stiffly Beaten Egg Whites

Be very careful not to get even a speck of egg yolk in the whites. Even a drop of egg yolk will prevent the whites from stiffening. And always use clean beaters. Any residual fat or oil will prevent the whites from fluffing up. You can use a drop of vinegar or lemon juice to help them stiffen.

1. Mix together the ground nuts, sugar, and butter. Prepare a springform pan with nonstick spray. Press the nut mixture into the bottom to form a crust, and chill.

2. Preheat the oven to 350°F.

3. Beat the egg whites until stiff and set aside.

4. Using an electric mixer, beat the cream cheese, sour cream, sugar, brown rice flour, salt, and egg yolks, adding the yolks one at a time. Beat in the lemon juice and lemon rind.

5. Gently fold in the egg whites. Pour the cheese-lemon mixture into the prepared springform pan. Bake for 1 hour. Turn off oven and crack the door, letting cool for another hour. Chill before serving. The chopped nuts and thinly sliced lemon make a nice touch.

Molten Lava Dark Chocolate Cake

*For such an easy recipe, it comes off as elegant. It just tastes more complex than it is to make.
The nice thing is that chestnut flour gives a wonderful underlying flavor.*

INGREDIENTS | SERVES 8

8 teaspoons butter, to grease custard cups

8 tablespoons sugar, to coat buttered custard cups

8 ounces semisweet baking chocolate

6 ounces unsalted butter

3 eggs

3 egg yolks

⅓ cup sugar

1 tablespoon arrowroot starch or tapioca starch

1 teaspoon vanilla extract

1 quart raspberry sorbet

1. Prepare the insides of eight (6-ounce) custard cups with 8 teaspoons of butter and 8 tablespoons of sugar. Preheat the oven to 425°F.

2. Over very low heat, melt the chocolate and 6 ounces of butter in a heavy saucepan.

3. In a large bowl, beat the eggs, egg yolks, sugar, starch, and vanilla for about 10 minutes. Add the chocolate mixture by the tablespoonful until the eggs have "digested" some of the chocolate. Fold in the rest of the chocolate-butter mixture.

4. Divide the mixture between the custard cups. Place the cups on a cookie sheet and bake for 12–13 minutes. The sides should be puffed and the center very soft. Serve hot with raspberry sorbet spooned into the "craters."

Raspberry Coulis

You can really use any berry in this recipe. Heavily seeded berries can be strained though a fine sieve or cheesecloth.

INGREDIENTS | MAKES 1½ CUPS

1 pint raspberries

½ cup sugar

¼ cup water or orange juice

Place the berries in a saucepan with the sugar and water or juice. Bring to a boil. Cool and strain.

Molten Sweet White Chocolate Cake

This is delicious with fresh berries and whipped cream spooned into the "craters."

INGREDIENTS | SERVES 8

8 teaspoons butter, to grease custard cups

8 tablespoons sugar, to coat buttered custard cups

8 ounces unsweetened white baking chocolate

6 ounces unsalted butter

3 eggs

3 egg yolks

⅓ cup sugar

1 tablespoon arrowroot starch or tapioca starch

1 teaspoon vanilla extract

½ teaspoon salt

2 cups mixed berries (such as strawberries, raspberries, and blueberries)

1. Prepare the insides of eight (6-ounce) custard cups with 8 teaspoons butter and 8 tablespoons sugar. Preheat the oven to 425°F.

2. Melt the white chocolate and butter in a heavy saucepan over low heat.

3. In a large bowl, using an electric mixer, beat together the eggs, egg yolks, sugar, and starch. Add the vanilla and salt.

4. Keep beating and slowly add, by the tablespoonful, one-fourth of the white-chocolate mixture. When well blended, add the rest of the white-chocolate mixture, very slowly.

5. Divide between the custard cups, place on a cookie sheet, and bake for about 12 minutes. Serve with mixed berries in the "craters." You can also vary this by using shaved bittersweet chocolate in the craters, or you can spoon in ice cream or sorbet.

Orange Carrot Cake

This delicious cake has a nice zing with the addition of a little lemon juice and the grated orange rind. The gingerroot adds an appealing sophistication, so go ahead and impress your friends.

INGREDIENTS | SERVES 8–10

4 eggs, separated

½ cup brown sugar

1½ cups grated carrots

1 tablespoon lemon juice

Grated rind of ½ fresh orange

½ cup brown rice flour or sorghum flour

1" fresh gingerroot, peeled and minced or 2 teaspoons ground ginger

1½ teaspoons baking soda

½ teaspoon salt

What's Up, Doc?

Carrot cake was created during World War II when flour and sugar were rationed. The sweetness of carrots contributed to this cake, and when oranges were available, it became a feast. Cooks used their fuel carefully too, baking and making stews and soups in the oven all at the same time. Sometimes, hard times make for sweet endings.

1. Liberally butter a springform pan and preheat the oven to 325°F.

2. Beat the egg whites until stiff and set aside.

3. Beat the egg yolks, brown sugar, and carrots together. Add lemon juice, orange rind, and flour. When smooth, add the gingerroot, baking soda, and salt. Gently fold in the egg whites.

4. Pour the batter into the springform pan and bake for 1 hour. Test by plunging a toothpick into the center of the cake—if the pick comes out clean, the cake is done.

Stovetop Oatmeal Fudge Cookies

*You may know these cookies as "Preacher Cookies," "Stovetop Cookies," "Oatmeal Fudgies,"
or "No Bake Cookies." This is basically a recipe for fudge (technically a candy)
but with added peanut butter and oatmeal. If you need cookies fast, these are the way to go!*

INGREDIENTS | SERVES 24–30

½ cup (1 stick) butter

2 cups sugar

½ cup milk

½ cup baking cocoa

1 teaspoon vanilla extract

½ cup peanut butter

2 cups certified gluten-free quick-cook oats

Make Them Dairy-Free

You can make these cookies dairy-free by using ⅓ cup coconut oil or ⅓ cup spectrum palm shortening in place of the butter (you use less because butter contains some milk/liquid) and your favorite nondairy milk, such as almond milk or cashew milk, in place of dairy milk.

1. Line 2 or 3 cookie sheets with parchment paper and set aside. Melt butter in a medium-size saucepan over medium heat. Add sugar, milk, and cocoa to the butter and whisk to remove any lumps.

2. Continue to cook over medium-high heat until mixture is simmering. Cook for an additional 6–7 minutes, stirring constantly to prevent the mixture from burning. Remove from heat.

3. Add vanilla extract and peanut butter and stir until peanut butter has dissolved into the hot mixture. Quickly stir in the gluten-free oats.

4. Working quickly (as the mixture will harden as it sets), drop cookie mixture 1 tablespoon at a time onto the parchment paper. You will generally have enough batter to make 24–30 cookies.

5. Allow cookies to cool completely before serving or moving to a storage container. Cookies should be somewhat soft but hard enough so that they can be picked up and held. Store cookies at room temperature in an airtight container between sheets of parchment paper or plastic wrap so they don't stick together.

Chocolate Meringue and Nut Cookies

These are crisp and delicious, and the nuts add a wonderful crunch.
You can use almonds instead of the hazelnuts if you prefer.

INGREDIENTS | MAKES ABOUT 40 COOKIES

½ cup sugar, divided

¼ cup unsweetened cocoa powder

⅛ teaspoon salt

3 egg whites (from extra-large eggs)

⅛ teaspoon cream of tartar

½ cup coarsely chopped hazelnuts, lightly toasted

Ugly, but Good!

These cookies are known in Italy as "ugly but good"! Other, kinder descriptions include "kisses" and "crisps." They are a bit dumpy looking, but just try one. This recipe is a simplification of the original, far more time-consuming one.

1. Preheat the oven to 275°F. Line two cookie sheets with parchment paper.

2. Sift ¼ cup of the sugar and all of the cocoa together in a bowl. Add salt.

3. In a separate bowl, beat the eggs whites with the cream of tartar. When peaks begin to form, add the remaining ¼ cup sugar, a teaspoon at a time. Slowly beat in the cocoa mixture. The meringue should be stiff and shiny.

4. Add the chopped nuts. Drop by teaspoonfuls on the parchment paper. Bake for 45–50 minutes. Cool on baking sheets. You can place these in an airtight cookie tin or serve them the same day.

Indian Pudding

If you make too much, let any extra pudding firm up and fry it in butter for sweet griddle cakes for breakfast the next day.

INGREDIENTS | SERVES 8

4 cups milk, divided

¼ cup white or yellow gluten-free cornmeal (such as Bob's Red Mill)

⅓ cup dark brown sugar

¼ cup white sugar

1 teaspoon salt

1 teaspoon cinnamon

¼ teaspoon ground nutmeg

1 teaspoon minced fresh gingerroot

¼ cup molasses

Unsalted butter or nonstick spray, for baking dish

1. Preheat the oven to 250°F. Heat 2 cups of the milk.

2. Place the cornmeal, sugars, salt, cinnamon, nutmeg, gingerroot, and molasses in the top of a double boiler.

3. Whisk the hot milk into the mixture, cooking and stirring over simmering water for 10 minutes or until smooth.

4. Prepare a baking dish with butter or nonstick spray.

5. Whisk the remaining cold milk into the hot mixture and pour into the baking dish. Bake for 3 hours. Serve hot or at room temperature with whipped cream.

Strawberry Clouds

These fluffy delights are cool and refreshing. Garnish with sprigs of mint.
The recipe is a cross between a Bavarian cream and a mousse.

INGREDIENTS | SERVES 4

1 (¼-ounce) package unflavored gelatin
¼ cup cold water
1 cup boiling water
1 pint strawberries, rinsed and hulled
Sugar, to taste
2 egg whites, beaten stiff
½ cup heavy cream, beaten stiff with 1 tablespoon sugar

Clouds

You can use berries as a flavoring for clouds, but peaches, blanched and mashed, are also very good, as are pears. Try making a cloud with fresh, spicy applesauce for fall. The basic principle works with all fruits. Just vary the amount of sugar to suit the type of fruit; that is, if the fruit is very sweet, use less sugar.

1. Place the gelatin and cold water in the jar of your blender. Let stand for 5 minutes before blending so the gelatin can "bloom." With the motor running, slowly pour in the boiling water.

2. Add strawberries and sugar and process until smooth, stopping to scrape down the sides of the jar.

3. When the berries have cooled, fold in the egg whites and whipped cream. Refrigerate until chilled, mixing occasionally.

Blueberry-Peach Cobbler

This smells and tastes like August. You might not think peaches and blueberries would pair well together, but this cobbler proves the combination is a winner.

INGREDIENTS | SERVES 10

6 ripe peaches, blanched in boiling water, skinned, pitted, and sliced

½ cup fresh lemon juice

1 cup sugar, divided

1 pint blueberries, rinsed and picked over, stems removed

½ cup (1 stick) unsalted butter, melted

½ teaspoon salt

1½ cups brown rice flour

1 tablespoon baking powder

1 cup buttermilk or 1 cup milk or nondairy milk plus 1 tablespoon lemon juice

1. Preheat the oven to 375°F.

2. Slice peaches into a bowl and sprinkle with lemon juice and ½ cup of the sugar. Add the blueberries and mix well.

3. Prepare a 9" × 13" baking dish with nonstick spray. Spread the peaches and blueberries on the bottom. Pour the melted butter into a large bowl. Add the remaining ½ cup sugar and salt and whisk in the flour and baking powder. Add the buttermilk and stir; don't worry about lumps.

4. Drop the batter by tablespoonfuls over the fruit. Bake for 35–40 minutes. Cool for 25 minutes. Serve with vanilla ice cream or whipped cream.

Espresso Custard

This silky, rich custard can be served with whipped cream or coffee ice cream.

INGREDIENTS | SERVES 4

3 tablespoons instant espresso powder

2 tablespoons boiling water

2 cups whipping cream

3 eggs

4 teaspoons cornstarch

4 teaspoons cold water

½ cup sugar, or to taste

1 teaspoon vanilla extract

Espresso

Espresso coffee beans are roasted longer than the beans for regular coffee; that's why they have such a dark and deep flavor. In cooking, use instant espresso powder, and you certainly can use decaf espresso powder for equally good results, with no caffeine buzz.

1. Preheat the oven to 325°F. Whisk together the espresso powder and boiling water, add the cream, and beat in the eggs. In a separate bowl, whisk the cornstarch and water together until smooth and beat into the espresso mixture.

2. Add the rest of the ingredients and stir well. Place four buttered (6-ounce) custard cups in a roasting pan of hot water in the middle of the oven. Add the custard.

3. Bake for 50–60 minutes. Serve warm, at room temperature, or chilled with whipped cream.

Apple Brown Betty with Cornbread

In the early days of the United States, no food went to waste. Thus, stale bread was made into a delicious, homey baked pudding. You can achieve the same goal in your dorm with this recipe!

INGREDIENTS | SERVES 4

4 large tart apples, peeled, cored, and sliced

Juice of ½ lemon

2 cups cubed gluten-free cornbread

2 eggs, lightly beaten

1½ cups milk

1 teaspoon vanilla extract

¼ teaspoon ground nutmeg

1 teaspoon ground cinnamon

⅛ teaspoon ground cloves

½ teaspoon salt

½ cup dark brown sugar, or to taste

½ cup (1 stick) butter

1. Preheat the oven to 350°F. Liberally butter a 2-quart casserole dish or prepare it with nonstick spray.

2. Put the apples in the casserole dish and sprinkle with lemon juice. Add the cornbread cubes. Mix well.

3. In a bowl, beat together the eggs, milk, vanilla, spices, salt, and brown sugar. Add mixture to the apples and cornbread cubes. Dot with butter.

4. Bake for 45 minutes or until brown on top and very moist inside. Serve warm with whipped cream or ice cream.

Why Not Use Canned Whipped Cream?

Whipped cream that comes in aerosol spray cans is much sweeter than the cream you would whip yourself. Also, there is more air than cream, so you are paying a premium for the spray convenience. When you do your own cream whipping, you will get a lot more flavor, no additives, and a healthier end product.

Raspberry "Parfait"

This is a great choice on those evenings when you don't want to serve anything too heavy for dessert. But if you just can't resist the sweet stuff, top with a few chocolate sprinkles.

INGREDIENTS | SERVES 2

1 cup regular or dairy-free vanilla ice cream

3 teaspoons lime juice

2 teaspoons sugar

1 cup frozen raspberries

In a blender, blend together the ice cream, lime juice, and sugar. Add the frozen fruit and process again. Pour into two parfait or tall drinking glasses. Serve immediately or freeze.

Perfect Parfait

Did you know that the word *parfait* is French for "perfect"? In the United States, November 25 has been designated as National Parfait Day.

Basic Rice Krispies Squares

Looking for a late-night study snack? This simple treat takes mere minutes to make and only requires a hot plate.

INGREDIENTS | MAKES ABOUT 24 SQUARES

⅓ cup butter or margarine

4½ cups mini marshmallows

6 cups Kellogg's Gluten-Free Rice Krispies cereal

1. In a heavy frying pan, melt the butter or margarine and marshmallows over low heat (if the heat is too high, the melted marshmallow will stick to the pan). When the marshmallows have completely melted, remove from heat.

2. Stir in the cereal and mix thoroughly. Spread out the mixture evenly in a 9" × 13" pan. Serve warm, or cool in the refrigerator for 1 hour first. Cut into squares before serving.

Orange Cornmeal Cookies

This is an adaptation of a classic Italian cookie. You and your friends will love them. Use your favorite flavor additions, such as currants, dried cranberries, raisins, or dried apple chips.

INGREDIENTS | MAKES 30 COOKIES

3 eggs

1 cup sugar

1½ cups gluten-free yellow cornmeal (such as Bob's Red Mill)

1¼ cups brown rice flour

½ teaspoon salt

¾ teaspoon xanthan gum

¾ cup (1½ sticks) unsalted butter, melted

1 tablespoon concentrated orange juice

Zest of ½ orange, very finely minced

1. Process the eggs and sugar in a food processor. Slowly add the rest of the ingredients and continue to process, stopping occasionally to scrape the bowl. Don't overprocess.

2. When the dough comes together, remove from the food processor and place in plastic wrap. Refrigerate for 1–2 hours.

3. Preheat the oven to 350°F. Prepare a cookie sheet with nonstick spray or parchment paper.

4. Shape the dough into a flat oval. Break off a small piece and roll into a ball. Flatten and place on cookie sheet to make one cookie. Repeat until all of the dough is used. Bake for 10 minutes or until golden.

Lemon Cranberry Sorbet

This easy sorbet makes a refreshing midafternoon or evening snack. Feel free to skip the final freezing if you're in a hurry. It just means the fruit won't have the firm, grainy texture of a sorbet.

INGREDIENTS | SERVES 1

1 cup (about 48) cranberries, washed and drained

½ teaspoon grated fresh ginger (optional)

¾ cup water, divided

4 tablespoons sugar

2 tablespoons lemon juice

1. Place the cranberries, ginger (if using), and ½ cup of the water in a small saucepan. Cook over medium heat until the cranberries pop, about 5–6 minutes. Gently mash the cranberries.

2. Stir in the remaining water, sugar, and lemon juice. Bring to a boil, stirring constantly. Remove from the heat and let cool. Pour into a serving bowl and place in the freezer until the sorbet is just starting to freeze, about 30 minutes.

3. Place in a blender or food processor and process until smooth. Freeze again.

Speedy Mocha "Mousse" Pudding

Instant pudding takes the work out of making this tasty mousse.

INGREDIENTS | SERVES 4–6

2 cups heavy whipping cream
½ cup brewed instant coffee
½ cup confectioners' sugar
½ cup unsweetened cocoa powder
1 teaspoon vanilla extract
1 package instant vanilla pudding
½ cup prepared whipped cream, or to taste
4–6 maraschino cherries

1. Combine the first 6 ingredients in a blender. Blend on low speed (prepare in 2 batches if necessary).

2. Transfer to parfait glasses and let sit for 5 minutes to allow the pudding to set.

3. Just before serving, top each parfait with whipped cream and a maraschino cherry.

Mocha Shake

For best results, use high-quality ice cream and your favorite coffee in this recipe.

INGREDIENTS | MAKES 2 CUPS

2 cups vanilla ice cream
1 cup cold brewed coffee
2 teaspoons unsweetened cocoa powder
2 ice cubes, crushed

Blend the ice cream, coffee, and cocoa powder in a blender. Add the ice cubes and process again. Chill until ready to serve.

Frozen Cappuccino Dessert

This tastes delicious served with whipped cream on top.

INGREDIENTS | SERVES 1

1 cup cold brewed coffee
2 tablespoons plain cream cheese
1 tablespoon sugar
2 teaspoons unsweetened cocoa powder

Combine all the ingredients in a blender and blend until smooth. Freeze for 2 hours, stirring occasionally. Serve chilled.

Mascarpone Pudding

The secret to this dessert lies in slowly cooking the rice until the grains are tender. Ricotta cheese can be substituted for the mascarpone.

INGREDIENTS | SERVES 6–8

1½ cups milk
1 cup long-grain rice
½ teaspoon ground cinnamon
1 teaspoon vanilla extract
¾ cup heavy cream
3 tablespoons sugar
1 cup mascarpone
16–20 whole almonds

1. In a medium-size saucepan, combine the milk and the rice. Stir in the cinnamon. Bring to a boil, uncovered, over medium heat. Cover, reduce heat to low, and simmer until cooked through, stirring occasionally.

2. In a bowl, stir the vanilla extract into the heavy cream. Add to the rice, stirring to combine. Continue cooking over low heat until the rice is tender. Remove from the heat.

3. Stir in the sugar and mascarpone. Spoon into dessert dishes and chill. Garnish with almonds.

Banana Mousse

Garnish each serving with one or two extra banana slices and sprinkle with nutmeg if desired.

INGREDIENTS | SERVES 6–8

3 large bananas, mashed

2 cups whipping cream

3 tablespoons confectioners' sugar

2 tablespoons lemon juice

¼ teaspoon ground nutmeg, or to taste

1 tablespoon rum, optional

Mousse Is a Must

Mousse is a form of creamy dessert typically made from egg and cream, usually in combination with other flavors such as chocolate or fruit. This recipe, which uses whipped cream, is a bit of a shortcut but no less delicious.

1. Purée the bananas in a blender.

2. Whip the cream at medium-high speed until it forms high peaks. Add the confectioners' sugar and whip briefly until it forms soft peaks (the mixture should be light and fluffy).

3. Fold the whipped cream into the mashed banana. Carefully stir in the lemon juice, nutmeg, and rum, if using. Spoon into parfait glasses.

Summer Fruit Compote

This delicious fruit compote is great on a chilly spring morning or a cool summer evening.

INGREDIENTS | MAKES 2 CUPS

2 medium bananas

⅓ cup sugar

1 cup water

1 teaspoon grated fresh ginger

¼ cup lemon juice

4 (5") cinnamon sticks

3 cups dried tropical fruit

1. Peel and slice the bananas.

2. Heat the sugar and water in a saucepan over low heat, stirring to dissolve sugar. Add ginger, lemon juice, and cinnamon sticks. Increase heat to medium and bring to a boil. Reduce heat to low and simmer for 5 minutes. Add dried fruit and bananas. Return to a boil. Reduce heat to low, cover, and simmer until the dried fruit is tender. Remove the cinnamon sticks.

3. Let cool briefly and serve warm, or refrigerate overnight and serve cold.

Soft Gingersnap Cookies

The warming aroma of this spicy cookie is enough to draw everyone into the kitchen to see what's baking. These cookies work best if you refrigerate the dough for an hour before baking them.

INGREDIENTS | MAKES 48 COOKIES

¾ cup butter, softened

1 cup sugar

1 large egg

¼ cup molasses

1 cup brown rice flour

¾ cup sorghum flour

¾ cup arrowroot starch or tapioca starch

1 teaspoon xanthan gum

1 teaspoon baking soda

2 teaspoons ground ginger

¾ teaspoon ground cinnamon

½ teaspoon ground cloves

¼ teaspoon salt

Additional sugar for rolling the cookies in

1. Preheat the oven to 350°F. Line baking sheets with parchment paper. Set aside.

2. In a stand mixer, beat the butter and sugar until light and fluffy. Add in the egg and molasses. Mix until blended.

3. In a mixing bowl, whisk together the brown rice flour, sorghum flour, arrowroot starch or tapioca starch, xanthan gum, baking soda, ginger, cinnamon, cloves, and salt.

4. Gradually add the dry ingredients to the butter mixture, mixing until well blended.

5. Cover and refrigerate dough for 1 hour.

6. Roll the dough into ¾" balls and roll to coat in the additional sugar. Place on baking sheet, 2" apart.

7. Bake in preheated oven for 10–12 minutes or until puffy and lightly browned. Remove to wire racks to cool. Store in an airtight container once completely cool.

Blueberry Mango Crisp

The topping on this crisp can be used on any kind of fresh fruit crisp.
If you cannot tolerate gluten-free oats, you can substitute quinoa flakes for them.

Tip for Easy Cleanup

Place the 8" × 8" baking dish on a larger cookie sheet to bake. That way, if your fruit juice bubbles over while baking, it will not fall to the bottom of your oven, and cleanup will be much easier.

1. Preheat the oven to 350°F.

2. In a large bowl, stir together the granulated sugar, cornstarch, and 1 teaspoon cinnamon. Add the diced mango, blueberries, and vanilla. Stir to coat the fruit with the sugar mixture. Pour into an 8" × 8" baking dish and set aside.

3. To make the crisp topping, stir together the oats, brown rice flour, brown sugar, ½ teaspoon cinnamon, and pinch of nutmeg. Using a pastry cutter or two knives, cut the cold butter into the oat-flour mixture until large crumbs, about the size of a pea, remain.

4. Sprinkle the crisp topping over the top of the fruit in the baking dish, and spread to create an even layer.

5. Bake in preheated oven for 40–45 minutes or until the fruit is hot and bubbly.

6. Remove from oven and allow to cool for at least 15 minutes before serving, as the fruit sauce is very hot straight out of the oven. This is delicious served warm with a scoop of vanilla ice cream.

Pumpkin Cheesecake

This dessert is the perfect combination of cheesecake and pumpkin pie.
This is a great dessert to enjoy during fall celebrations.

INGREDIENTS | SERVES 9

¾ cup crushed Cinnamon Chex cereal or gluten-free graham cracker crumbs

½ cup ground pecans

2 tablespoons granulated sugar

2 tablespoons brown sugar

¼ cup butter, melted

¾ cup granulated sugar

¾ cup pumpkin purée (not pie filling)

3 egg yolks

1½ teaspoons ground cinnamon

½ teaspoon ground nutmeg

½ teaspoon ground ginger

¼ teaspoon salt

3 (8-ounce) packages cream cheese

⅜ cup granulated sugar

1 large egg

1 egg yolk

2 tablespoons whipping cream

1 tablespoon cornstarch

1 teaspoon vanilla extract

Whole pecans and a jar of dulce de leche, for toppings (optional)

Keeping Things Clean

To keep your oven clean when baking anything in a springform pan, place the pan on a foil-lined baking sheet. This way, if the pan does not seal properly and some of the batter leaks out, it will not fall onto the bottom of your oven.

1. Preheat the oven to 350°F.

2. Combine the cereal or graham cracker crumbs, ground pecans, 2 tablespoons granulated sugar, 2 tablespoons brown sugar, and the melted butter and mix well. Firmly press into a 9" springform pan.

3. Combine ¾ cup granulated sugar, pumpkin purée, 3 egg yolks, spices, and salt in a medium bowl. Mix well and set aside.

4. In a separate bowl, beat the cream cheese with an electric mixer until light and fluffy; gradually add ⅜ cup granulated sugar and mix well. Add the whole egg, remaining egg yolk, and whipping cream, beating well. Add cornstarch and vanilla extract, and beat batter until smooth. Add pumpkin purée mixture and mix well. Pour batter over crust in springform pan.

5. Bake in preheated oven for 50–55 minutes. Do not overbake. The center may be soft but it will firm up when chilled. At this point, turn the oven off, and open the oven door, but leave the cake in the oven for the next hour. This will help prevent the top from cracking.

6. Cover and refrigerate until ready to serve. Remove the springform pan and, if desired, decorate the top of the cake with whole pecans and dulce de leche a few hours before serving. Refrigerate until ready to serve.

Oatmeal Chocolate Chip Cookies

These big, soft oatmeal cookies are loaded with chocolate chips.
To change things up a bit, feel free to use chopped nuts or different flavored baking chips,
such as cinnamon or butterscotch, in place of some of the chocolate chips.

INGREDIENTS | MAKES 48 COOKIES

1 cup (2 sticks) butter or margarine, softened

2 cups packed brown sugar

2 large eggs

1 teaspoon vanilla extract

1½ cups brown rice flour

¾ cup arrowroot starch or tapioca starch

½ teaspoon xanthan gum

1 teaspoon baking powder

½ teaspoon baking soda

2 cups certified gluten-free quick-cook oats

2 cups gluten-free chocolate chips

Freezing Cookies

These cookies freeze remarkably well. Just place in an airtight container and they keep in the freezer for 3–4 weeks. However, you can also freeze the dough before baking! Scoop dough onto a wax paper–lined baking sheet and place in freezer. Once cookies are completely frozen, you can place them in a resealable freezer bag. Frozen dough should be used within 4–6 weeks. To bake frozen cookies, place cookies on parchment-lined baking sheets, and let the dough come to room temperature before baking.

1. Preheat the oven to 350°F.

2. Cream together the softened butter or margarine and the brown sugar.

3. Add eggs, one at a time. Mix until blended. Stir in vanilla.

4. In a large bowl, combine brown rice flour, arrowroot starch or tapioca starch, xanthan gum, baking powder, and baking soda. Stir to blend.

5. Stir dry ingredients into butter-sugar mixture.

6. Add the oats and chocolate chips, and stir to combine all ingredients.

7. Using a cookie scoop (or two tablespoons), drop cookies onto parchment-lined cookie sheets. Bake cookies in preheated oven for 11–12 minutes or until they are slightly brown around the outside but still slightly moist in the middle.

8. Allow to cool on cookie sheet for 5 minutes before transferring to a wire rack.

9. Cool completely before storing in an airtight container.

White Cake

Every well-stocked recipe collection should have a recipe for a white cake.
Let this recipe for this fluffy cake be yours.

INGREDIENTS | SERVES 15

1½ cups brown rice flour

¾ cup arrowroot starch or tapioca starch

1 teaspoon xanthan gum

1½ cups sugar

2 teaspoons baking powder

1 teaspoon baking soda

½ teaspoon salt

½ cup (1 stick) unsalted butter, softened

¾ cup milk

2 teaspoons vanilla extract

4 egg whites

1. Preheat the oven to 350°F. Spray a 13" × 9" pan with nonstick cooking spray and set aside.

2. In a large bowl, combine brown rice flour, arrowroot starch or tapioca starch, xanthan gum, sugar, baking powder, baking soda, and salt and mix well with a whisk.

3. In a stand mixer fitted with a paddle attachment, beat the butter until fluffy. Add the flour mixture, along with the milk and vanilla. Beat until blended, and then beat on medium speed for 2 minutes.

4. Add the unbeaten egg whites, all at once, and beat 2 minutes longer. Pour batter into prepared pan. Bake 35–40 minutes or until cake is beginning to pull away from edges and is light golden brown. Cool completely on wire rack.

Crustless Pumpkin Pie

This pie has the same fantastic flavor as traditional pumpkin pie,
only it is much easier to make since it does not have a crust.

INGREDIENTS | SERVES 8

1 (15-ounce) can pumpkin purée (not pie filling)
½ cup packed brown sugar
½ cup granulated sugar
⅛ teaspoon ground cloves
½ tablespoon ground cinnamon
1 teaspoon ground ginger
½ teaspoon salt
2 teaspoons baking powder
½ cup sorghum flour
2 tablespoons tapioca starch
2 teaspoons vanilla extract
2 tablespoons olive oil
2 large eggs, beaten
½ cup evaporated milk
½ cup heavy cream
Whipped cream, for topping

1. Preheat the oven to 350°F.

2. Grease a 9½" pie plate with oil.

3. In a large bowl, combine all the ingredients and mix until well combined.

4. Pour into prepared pie plate, and bake in preheated oven for 60–70 minutes. The pie is done when a knife inserted into the middle comes out clean.

5. Cool completely before serving. Serve with a dollop of whipped cream.

The Skinny on Crustless Pies

Go ahead and have that scoop of whipped cream with your pie! By removing the crust from this pie, you save nearly 1,000 calories per pie, or 125 calories per slice.

Mango Creamsicle Sorbet

When the weather is hot and you're looking for a cold, refreshing treat, try this homemade sorbet recipe.

INGREDIENTS | SERVES 6

3 cups peeled, chopped mangoes or peaches
½ cup cold water
1 cup shredded coconut
2 tablespoons lemon juice

Sorbet

Try this recipe with other favorite fruits. If the sorbet does not seem sweet enough, add honey to the mixture next time. There is none added here because mango has a high sugar content on its own.

1. In a food processor or blender, combine mangoes or peaches and water; cover and process until smooth.

2. Add coconut and lemon juice; cover and process until smooth.

3. Transfer to container and freeze until solid, about 2 hours.

Delicious Pumpkin Pudding

This pumpkin pudding is a great dessert for the holidays. This recipe also offers a dairy-free alternative to the crustless pumpkin pie shared in this chapter.

INGREDIENTS | SERVES 8

2 large eggs

1 teaspoon cinnamon

½ teaspoon nutmeg

½ teaspoon cloves

½ teaspoon ginger

¾ cup sugar

1 (15-ounce) can organic pure pumpkin purée (not pumpkin pie filling)

1 (13.5-ounce) can coconut milk

½ cup crushed pecans

1. Preheat the oven to 375°F. Grease an 8" × 8" square baking pan.

2. Whisk the eggs in a medium bowl. Add the spices and sugar and whisk again.

3. Add the pumpkin and coconut milk and mix thoroughly.

4. Pour batter into prepared pan, top with pecans, and bake for 45 minutes.

Pumpkin: A Starchy Carbohydrate

Pumpkin is a fruit but should be considered a complex carbohydrate. It will raise your insulin levels when eaten. Pumpkin is always best eaten after exercise or when the sugar will be used to replenish glycogen storage. For that reason, eating high-glycemic-load items at bedtime is not recommended.

Keys to a Gluten-Free Diet

According to the Gluten Intolerance Group (*www .gluten.net*) and the American Dietetic Association, the following grains, flours, and starches are allowed in a gluten-free diet:

- Amaranth
- Arrowroot
- Bean
- Buckwheat
- Corn
- Millet
- Nut
- Potato
- Quinoa
- Rice
- Sorghum
- Soy
- Tapioca
- Tef

The following grains contain gluten and are not allowed:

- Barley
- Farina
- Kamut
- Oats (However, many companies now offer certified gluten-free oats that are grown in safe fields and processed in safe facilities. If you can tolerate oats, make sure to purchase certified gluten-free brands, such as Bob's Red Mill, Cream Hill Estates, or Jules Gluten-Free Oats. NOTE: Bob's Red Mill brand is not certified officially by the Gluten Intolerance Group, but they are tested to meet gluten-free safe standards of less than 10 parts per million.)
- Rye
- Spelt
- Triticale
- Wheat (durum, semolina)

The following ingredients are questionable and should not be consumed unless you can verify that they neither contain nor are derived from prohibited grains:

- Brown rice syrup (frequently made with barley)
- Dextrin (usually corn, but may be derived from wheat)
- Flour or cereal products
- Hydrolyzed vegetable protein (HVP), vegetable protein, hydrolyzed plant protein (HPP), or textured vegetable protein (TVP)
- Malt or malt flavoring (usually made from barley; okay if made from corn)
- Modified food starch or modified starch

- Natural and artificial flavors (However, extracts such as vanilla, orange, and lemon extracts are gluten-free.)

Additional components frequently overlooked that often contain gluten:

- Breading
- Coating mixes
- Communion wafers
- Croutons
- Imitation bacon
- Imitation seafood
- Marinades
- Pastas
- Processed meats
- Roux
- Sauces
- Self-basting poultry
- Soup bases
- Stuffing
- Thickeners

Online Resources

The Gluten-Free Mall

www.glutenfreemall.com

The Gluten-Free Mall was created by Scott Adams, who is better known in the celiac/gluten-free community for founding Celiac.com. On this site, you'll find high-quality gluten-free products.

The George Mateljan Foundation for the World's Healthiest Foods

www.whfoods.com

The George Mateljan Foundation for the World's Healthiest Foods was established by George Mateljan to discover, develop, and share scientifically proven information about the benefits of healthy eating. You can use the site's Recipe Assistant to search for recipes that exclude certain foods.

The Gluten Intolerance Group

www.gluten.net

The Gluten Intolerance Group, also known as GIG, is a 501(c)(3) nonprofit organization funded by private donations, including the Combined Federal Campaign, United Way Designated Giving, employer matching funds, proceeds from memberships, and the sale of products and educational resources.

Living Without

www.livingwithout.com

Living Without is a lifestyle guide for people with allergies and food sensitivities. It discusses a wide variety of health issues, including allergies; food sensitivities; multiple chemical sensitivities; wheat intolerance; gluten intolerance; lactose intolerance; dairy allergies; eating disorders; asthma; diabetes; dermatitis; gastroenterology-related disorders; diets that heal; celiac disease; anaphylaxis; and the common allergens of egg, dairy, wheat, peanuts, tree nuts, shellfish, fish, corn, soy, and gluten.

Glutenfreeda

www.glutenfreeda.com

The Glutenfreeda program was created to help people with celiac sprue disease learn to prepare all the foods they love, gluten-free. Their goal is to show the gluten-intolerant how to eat well, eat healthy, and function happily in a gluten-engorged world. Glutenfreeda recipes will be enjoyed by your entire family and were selected to make eating a delicious experience, not a sacrifice.

Ginger Lemon Girl

www.gingerlemongirl.com

This is a website started in 2007, written by Carrie Forbes, sharing easy and healthy gluten-free recipes and stories. Complete with a full (and free) gluten-free recipe index, gluten-free beginner's resources, cooking and baking tips, shopping tips, and a gluten-free support group, this website will provide recipes and support along your gluten-free journey.

Cooking Gluten-Free!
www.cookingglutenfree.com
Published by Celiac Publishing, Cooking Gluten-Free! is a labor of love designed to prove that gluten-free food can be excellent.

Rice and Recipes
www.riceandrecipes.com
This site includes recipes, recipe contests, rice links, and rice facts.

Gluten-Free Pantry
www.glutenfreepantry.com
This site includes recipes, a retail-store locator, and information on celiac disease, autism, and more.

Celiac Disease and Gluten-Free Diet Support Center
www.celiac.com/celiacdisease.html
This support center at Celiac.com provides important resources and information for people on gluten-free diets due to celiac disease, gluten intolerance, dermatitis herpetiformis, wheat allergy, or other health issues. Celiac.com offers key gluten- and wheat-free online resources that are helpful to anyone with special dietary needs.

The Gluten Free Trio
www.pamelasproducts.com/GFTrio.html
The Gluten Free Trio is a collaboration of three independent companies: Pamela's Products, Mrs. Leeper's Pasta, and Edward & Sons.

Gluten Solutions
www.glutensolutions.com
Buy food and get information.

Amazing Grains
www.amazinggrains.com
This site sells Montina flour, cookbooks, and bakeware, and also features a grower's co-op and support groups.

Enjoy Life Foods
www.enjoylifefoods.com
Visit this site to browse and buy, read food facts, and check out other resources.

Glossary of Basic Cooking Terms

baste: To spoon or brush a liquid over food—usually meat—during cooking. Basting prevents the food from drying out while being cooked. The basting liquid can be anything from a specially prepared sauce to the pan juices from meat that is cooking.

blanch: To plunge vegetables and other food briefly into boiling water. Blanching seals in the color and textures of tender-crisp vegetables, such as asparagus. It's also a quick and easy way to loosen the skins on nuts, tomatoes, and other fruit, and to remove the salty flavor from foods such as ham. Blanched food that isn't going to be cooked immediately should be plunged in ice-cold water. This "shocks" the food and stops the cooking process.

boil: To heat a liquid until bubbles form on the surface, or to cook food by placing it in liquid that is boiling. In a "rolling boil" the entire liquid is boiling, not just the surface. Stirring with a spoon won't cause the liquid to stop boiling.

braise: To cook meat with a small amount of liquid in a tightly covered pan. Usually, the meat is browned before braising. This cooking method is an easy way to tenderize cheaper cuts of meat.

broil: To cook food right above or under a heat source. Food can be broiled indoors in the oven or outdoors on a grill. When broiling meat, use a rack or broiling pan so that the fat from the meat can drain.

brown: To briefly fry meat in oil until it is browned on both sides but not cooked through. Browning the meat helps keep it tender by sealing in its natural juices.

caramelize: To heat sugar until it becomes golden and has a syrupy texture. Meat can be "caramelized" by heating it in a frying pan to draw out its natural juices, which brown—or "caramelize"—on the bottom of the pan.

chop: To cut food into small pieces, not necessarily of a uniform size. Garlic is frequently chopped before frying.

dice: To cut food into small cubes no larger than ¼".

drain: To remove the water from blanched, washed, rinsed, or boiled food. For hassle-free draining, purchase a colander. Depending on your budget, several varieties are available, from stainless steel to inexpensive plastic.

dredge: To coat food—usually meat or seafood—with a dry ingredient before frying. Depending on the recipe, the dry ingredient can be anything from flour or cornstarch to bread crumbs or cornmeal. Dredging provides a crisp coating and helps seal in flavor. For best results, food should be fried immediately after the coating is applied.

marinate: To soak food in a liquid before cooking, both to tenderize it and add flavor. Most marinades contain an acidic ingredient such as lemon juice, wine, or vinegar.

mince: To cut food into very small pieces. Minced food is cut more finely than chopped food.

sauté: To quickly cook food in a pan in a small amount of oil, butter, or other fat.

simmer: To cook food in liquid that is almost, but not quite, boiling.

steam: To cook food in the steam given off by boiling water. Unlike boiling, in steaming the food never comes into direct contact with the hot water.

Index

We Have

EVERYTHING®

on Anything!

The Everything® list spans a wide range of subjects, with more than 500 titles covering 25 different categories:

Business	History	Reference
Careers	Home Improvement	Religion
Children's Storybooks	Everything Kids	Self-Help
Computers	Languages	Sports & Fitness
Cooking	Music	Travel
Crafts and Hobbies	New Age	Wedding
Education/Schools	Parenting	Writing
Games and Puzzles	Personal Finance	
Health	Pets	